The Truth!

What if everything you've ever learned
about marketing your business was wrong?

John Mulry, MSc

What others are saying about John Mulry:

"John was lucky enough to be personally mentored and trained by me. As a GKIC Certified Business Advisor, he's equipped with an arsenal of tools that any small business owner can pick up and run with to start producing big time, bottom line results. This is exactly the kind of advice I needed when I started my career... but nobody who really knew what was going on was willing to share. If you're a business owner and you want real improvement in your business then I highly suggest you listen to what John has to say."
– Dan Kennedy, Dan Kennedy, Serial Entrepreneur, Multi Millionaire and Highest Paid Direct Response Marketer in the World

"The thing about John that most people aren't willing to do, is to actually apply the best practices that they learn to their own business and life in order to achieve maximum effectiveness in minimum time." **- Nick Nanton, CEO of the Dicks Nanton Celebrity Branding® Agency, Emmy Award Winning Director, Producer & Best-Selling Author**

"If someone had told me you will get an extra €10k in your bank account from doing this [working with John], I would have laughed but yes this has transformed my business and the results were outstanding. I closed a total of 24 clients once I activated what I had learned. It totally changed by way of thinking and how to approach my marketing strategy. The results were immediate. This has made a huge impact on my business going forward. I now have a system in place I have laser-targeted marketing and am no longer just "winging it". In 8 hours the amount of marketing information I didn't know that I didn't know was just ridiculous. A lot of my business comes through Facebook and primarily referrals. However on this workshop

I discovered exactly who my niche market are and that probably 50% of them aren't on facebook and probably don't know my current clients. Well what about my website? I asked. Well you can track that, John said. And then went on to explain how to drive that missing 50% from offline to online, reel them in to get their contact information and then to entice them over 28 days to get in contact with me. This is only one example of mattered to me and this only covered 2 modules out of the ten covered that day. I don't care who you are, unless you've studied marketing or already work with someone who does your marketing for you then it's probably safe to say your just winging it. Get on board and get the information."

- **John T Kenny, Access Fitness, Dublin**

"This book has literally transformed the way I think about marketing and the way I approach it. John's book is so digestible, so easy to read, it's nearly like you know the man. The way he communicates the information in the book is so easy to follow. He really puts you in the mindset of the buyer or prospect. John brings it back to simple techniques of what people want and what they need. My knowledge of marketing has greatly increased because of John's book The Truth. I've already applied it to my business and I know I'm going to be seeing results very soon. John guides you by the hand, takes you through the process. He really, really knows the psychology of buyers and this book will help your business grow, grow and grow. 10/10" ~
Aidan Corkey, Entrepreneur, Dublin, Ireland

"I have been in this industry for years. I felt a bit lost and just doing what everyone else was doing to try and generate revenue. I was becoming a follower and not a leader. I knew things weren't working but didn't know how to change it. This course gave me back that motivation and forced me to re-evaluate WHY I was in this industry.

But not just that it gave me the tools to make the necessary changes. I can't believe the results. The very next day after the course I reactivated my lapse clients and straight away I had 2 clients come back to me. In total I have an extra €1,100 in revenue a month"
– Alan Gibson

"I like how brutally honest you are. It's great to receive advice from someone who has had experience with these problems and triumphed!" **– Chloe H.**

"John Mulry you are god damn amazing, I hope this is included in the testimonial. You have changed my attitude; my daily life is now easier and more refreshing since I started with The Expect Success Academy team. You can't put into words how grateful and appreciative I am for all your attention and co-operation. You have put a smile and swagger back in my step, something which is priceless." **~ Kevin Nugent, Mr. Waffle, Galway Ireland**

"Doing John and Sean's course has given me the perspective and practical tools I need to implement plans to grow my business. My net growth since the course has risen to 30% a month. If you're on the fence about attending this course, then you need to seriously ask yourself why you're not prepared to invest a small fee to drive your business forward and achieve your goals when you're asking clients to invest a lot more to achieve theirs." **- *Phil Giffney***

For more testimonials as well as video testimonials visit: www.JohnMulry.com/testimonials

John Mulry, MSc

ISBN-13: 978-0-9928003-1-4

The Truth! is available at special quantity discounts for bulk purchases, for sales promotions, premiums, fundraising, and educational use. For more information, please write to the below address.

Published by: Expect Success Academy
Unit 14, Ballybane Enterprise Centre
Galway, Ireland

www.JohnMulry.com | www.GKIC.ie

First Edition, 2015

Edited by: Jessica Thompson
www.Jessica.ie

Cover Art by: Samwise

Published in Ireland

The Truth!

For Jess...

You're my reason why... my everything... and I'll love you always...

For Mam...

Thank you for all your continued support and forever kindness...

In life, you don't necessarily get what you want and you don't necessarily get what you need. Instead, you get what you honestly and truly believe you deserve. In other words, you get what you expect, so why not expect success?

–John Mulry

Check out the special invitation on page 152 to apply one of John's coaching, courses or done-for-you marketing campaigns…

About John Mulry

"Helping entrepreneurs grow their business and profits through successful online and offline direct marketing systems."

Biography:

John Mulry is an award winning trusted marketing advisor, lead generation, client experience specialist, author, speaker and is aptly known as the 'marketing maverick' by his clients and close friends. He offers strategies for business owners to grow their business through direct response marketing.

Leaving his unhappy life in the corporate finance world, he embarked on a journey from a year volunteering in South America, where he witnessed hardship, brutality and kindness side by side, to learning from and studying under some of the most world renowned experts in business, lifestyle and coaching.

When John first started his business rather than accept the status quo of the impending doom of the recession he sought out and has studied under some of the most world-renowned experts in business, direct response marketing and coaching. Experts including marketing legends Jay Abraham and Dan Kennedy, GKIC, lifestyle and business experts Tony Robbins, Dax Moy, and Emmy award winning movie Director/branding agent Nick Nanton.

He lives and breathes by his creeds "invest, consume and act" and having an "expect success attitude". John was handpicked by Dan Kennedy and is Ireland's only GKIC Certified Business Advisor.

John's mission is to show you how to:

- Attract more of your ideal customers and clients,
- Get them to come back more often,
- Have them spending more on each visit,
- Have them send you more referrals than you ever thought possible.

These strategies are revealed through his monthly workshops, his monthly Expect Success with Marketing Magazine, his various online/offline courses and resources, his full day & half day consultations and his monthly marketing and coaching programs,(by application only).

What separates John from other consultants/agencies?

- John's marketing and business growth systems are exactly that - systems. They are scalable, trackable, repeatable and profitable.
- The only thing that matters to John is results. Opinion doesn't matter, bright shiny objects don't matter. Direct response marketing is all about holding every Euro invested accountable to a direct result.

Contacting John

Should you wish to contact John directly concerning consulting, coaching, done-for-you marketing campaigns or speaking engagements please us the below contact details and have full contact details on hand at time of contacting.

Phone: +353874168050
Fax: +35391396397
Website: www.JohnMulry.com | www.GKIC.ie
Address: Unit 14, Ballybane Enterprise centre, Ballybane, Galway, Ireland.
Email: John@JohnMulry.com

The Truth!

Table of Contents

The Truth!

Introduction

"The value of an idea lies in the using of it."

- Thomas Edison

What I want to do in this book is teach you a system for marketing your business to a point where it becomes instantly obvious to your prospects that they would be an idiot to do business with anyone other than you at anytime, anywhere or at any price.

I want to show you how to leverage what you're already doing and how you can see massive results for your business. Just by changing the way you do all of your marketing and advertising.

And I'm not talking about radical changes. Just simple, common sense changes that enable you to exponentially leverage your marketing's results.

And I'm going to share with you EXACTLY how you can accomplish amazing results with your marketing and in the process, dominate your entire industry.

In this short but powerful book, I'm going to teach you how to achieve massive leverage with your marketing, meaning simply that you'll make more money for the same time, the same money, and the same effort you're expending right now.

Why will this enable you to dominate your local market? Simple... most businesses simply don't know how to do this. They don't understand the tremendous untapped potential that lies within their marketing.

Most businesses today spend money on marketing and advertising... and then decide that whatever results they get from that marketing is probably about as good as it's going to get. They realize that their results can fluctuate up and down, but they never imagine that the true results they can achieve.

I'm here to tell you point blank that nothing could be further from the truth. The marketing system I'm going to teach you in this book is based on unchanging principles of human nature that dictate that people always want to make the best buying decision possible, and therefore marketing's job -- your job -- is not to yak incessantly about how great you are or how low your prices are.

Your job is to position your prospective buyer's so they have total control over the decision-making process based on them having enough quantity and quality of information to determine that they're receiving the most value for the price they pay.

The system I'm going to teach you while not new in the global side of things, will truly be a breakthrough for your marketing and advertising, yet it's simple and easy to understand.

There are thousands of successes to prove that this works literally every time it's implemented properly, regardless of what business or industry you're in.

I'm going to introduce you to some very common-sense principles of marketing that you'll be able to instantly validate and embrace principles that will give you a clear vision of what your marketing is supposed to look like and, just as importantly, what it's not supposed to look like.

I want to show you the fundamental formulas and strategies to not only make your marketing work better but to enable you to create what we call "competition-crushing" marketing. I want you to see how powerful all of this is allow you to comprehend what the possibilities are for your business and what a significant advantage you'll hold over your competitors when you implement it.

If you feel that you need help implementing or acting upon what you read, do not hesitate to reach out to me and apply for my coaching, marketing training or my done-for-you marketing campaigns. Visit www.JohnMulry.com to get started.

John Mulry, MSc

The Truth!

What if everything you've ever learned about marketing your business was wrong?

"So often people are working hard at the wrong thing. Working on the right thing is probably more important than working hard."

- Caterina Fake

Everything you know about generating leads and growing your business is wrong. Now don't take offence to this statement. I'm not calling you out as a fool or an idiot and that you don't know anything. I'm not sitting here a top some pedestal saying I know everything. I'm merely suggesting that what you've learned about lead generation, marketing and growing your business is NOT the most effective way to do it.

There are two main components to any marketing plan: strategic marketing and tactical marketing. Strategic marketing is the content of your message.

It's what you say and how you say it, including the concepts that you choose to focus on, the words and images you use to communicate those concepts, and the tone in which the message is delivered.

Tactical marketing on the other hand, has to do with the execution of the strategic marketing such as placing ads, building a website, attending trade shows and things like that.

If I ask a business owner about their marketing plan, the answer almost always comes back in terms of tactical marketing: They're on Facebook, Twitter, they send direct mail, run radio and newspaper ads, and create a website... those kinds of things.

But the key to effective marketing is to master the strategic side not the tactical.

<u>What</u> you say in your marketing and <u>how</u> you say it are almost always more important than the marketing medium <u>where</u> you say it.

Both are important of course, but the real leverage is in the messaging itself and that's the strategic side of marketing. In fact, when a marketing campaign bombs, the tendency is almost always to blame the marketing medium like the newspaper or radio station, which is the tactical part of the plan, without any regard to how good or bad the <u>strategy</u> behind that marketing piece was.

During this book, you'll learn how to say things in a way that will make a profound difference in your marketing results.

The system and principles are not opinion or theory, they have been successfully implemented in over 400 different industries, including business coaches, social media consultants, print companies, design companies, home heating oil businesses, one man shows, contractors, business brokers, accountants, financial companies, retail stores, real estate companies, home builders, restaurants, coffee shops, software companies, doctors, dentists, remodelers, internet companies, manufacturing companies, and anything and everything else you can think of. It works with all sizes of businesses from start-ups... clear up to Fortune 500 companies.

These principles will let you finally quit competing on price and start selling your product or service for what you're really worth. You'll drive in more leads and often see an increase in your advertising response by 2 to more than 100 times.

You'll also convert a higher percentage of those leads and make your salespeople into superstars. You'll increase the amount of your average sale and your list of clients that pay, stay and refer will increase significantly. In short, you'll get a bigger bang for your marketing buck.

But maybe best of all, you will finally have total control over your marketing and lead generation results. Now in saying all of that, you may be thinking *"John, you're full of it"* and if you are thinking that, please quit that stinking thinking as Zig Ziglar used to say and ask yourself where's the profit in that? What profit do you get out of your negative thinking? None. So read on with an open mind, not a closed one, otherwise, maybe this book isn't for you. Now that my mini rant is over, let me ask you one simple question...

What is the actual purpose of marketing?

I mean, what is marketing really supposed to do? Well, in a nutshell, marketing is supposed to help facilitate your prospects' decision-making process.

There are prospects out there that need to buy what you sell. Sometimes they need to be educated to the fact that they need to buy what you sell in the first place, and other times... they already know that they want it but they need help deciding who they should buy it from.

Often, they think they might want what you sell, but they have questions and concerns that need to be overcome before they'll pull out their credit card or checkbook. But consider this.

Because these prospects are not experts in what you do... or their exposure to what you sell is quite low they don't really know the relevant issues surrounding the purchase.

They don't know how to make the best decision. They can't tell the difference between the best deal and a major mistake. Which leaves an opportunity for you to provide them with this information and then guide them through the buying process. **Consider this example.**

Throughout your life, how many conservatories have you ever bought? Have you bought five? Two? One? Or like 99% of homeowners... zero? Let's assume you fall in that group of 99% of people who have never bought a conservatory before. Do you have any idea whatsoever how to buy a conservatory? Can you tell the difference between a €10,000 conservatory and a €25,000 one just by looking at it?

Of course you can't. Now realize that when people need to buy what you sell, they are, generally speaking, just as clueless about what you're selling as you are about conservatories. So your job, simply put, is to facilitate your prospect's decision-making process. Listen, this is actually pretty simple.

All prospects and customers want the exact same things. And it really doesn't matter what type of business you have. They want to feel confident that their money has been well-spent... and that their decision has been made to the best of their ability.

They want to get the best deal. Not just the best price, but the best deal in terms of overall value. People instinctively want to make the best decision possible and not feel like they've got to second-guess their buying decision.

All you have to do as the marketer is figure out what's important to your prospects educate them as to what constitutes the best deal when it comes to buying what you sell. Remember value.

And then show them quantifiable proof that you actually provide the best deal in terms of price and value. All this has to be communicated to them in a way they'll pay attention to, believe in, and then take action on.

When this occurs, the prospect gets what they really want from you complete confidence that they have actually made the best decision possible and that they have truly gotten the best value. But here's the problem.

Instead of using marketing to educate and facilitate the decision-making process and build the case why a product or service is the best on the market most businesses fill their marketing with self-serving jargon that's only a thinly-veiled way to say, *"Buy it from me because I want you to give me the money instead of my competitor."*

That's why people become jaded and why they resist marketing. They tend to either dismiss your entire marketing message or worse they become skeptical and stop paying attention to the message altogether. Prospective buyers want and need to be educated so that they can feel confident when making their purchase decision and no one's providing it.

But here's the good news...

The first one who does provide prospects with this information wins all the most profitable customers available! When marketing is done improperly, the end result is 100% predictable: you start to feel intense pricing pressure from your prospects, and typically you're forced to cave in, lower your prices, destroy your margins, and make way less money than you should just to stay competitive.

And you get to spend more time at work and away from your family than those that are successful.

Here's the brutal truth and please don't be offended by this but if you're always competing on price, it's your own fault!

Your lack of marketing ability has led to a situation where there's no discernible difference between you and your competition. There have been no additional parameters... or relevant issues introduced to educate your prospects as to what really constitutes the best value when it comes to buying what you sell.

If you feel like you're always competing on price, it's because price is the only relevant variable that you've given your prospects to consider. From the prospect's perspective, all things appear equal, so they default to the business offering the lowest price.

I'm about to show you how to fix that once and for all. This book simply put is a step-by-step program for innovating and marketing your business. It will allow you to first, be better than the competition... and then second do better marketing than your competition.

This allows you to separate your business from your competition and become the obvious choice for your prospects to do business with.

Inside Perception and Outside Reality

Consider this there are actually two sides to your business: First, there's what I call the "inside reality," and second, what I call the "outside perception."

The inside reality encompasses everything you do and everything that makes your business great. It's all of your skills: the people who work for you, your expertise, the way you service your customers before, during, and after the sale.

It's your systems, your operational procedures, and your commitment to excellence. It's your passion... and the way you conduct your business on a daily basis. Add these all together and they equal your value to the marketplace. That's what I call the inside reality.

So how's your inside reality?

If you asked your customers why they buy from you, they could probably tell you something quantifiable, specific and instantly obvious. They could point to specific benefits they enjoy when doing business with you.

Then they would say things like... *"That's why I do business here, that's why I refer my friends to come here, and that's why I'm a loyal customer. That's why I'm willing to pay more here... and why I keep coming back."*

That's your inside reality. So your inside reality is all about what you do and what you are that allows you to perform better.

However, your outside perception has to do with how customers and prospects <u>perceive</u> your company. The outside perception is developed through the interactions that your prospects and customers have with your business.

Your customers will draw on their past buying experiences with you to form the outside perception of your business.

But here's the problem. If you provide unmatched and unequaled customer service... and your customers absolutely love you... none of that matters to your prospects if, number one, they don't even know you exist as an option... or number two, they see your marketing and advertising and, because of your inability to market your business properly, their perception is that you're no different, or no better, or no worse than your competitors.

I would estimate that well over 95% of all businesses are completely inept when it comes to marketing... and the end result is that your inside reality and your outside perception are perceived to be different.

You see, regardless of how good you are, regardless of your inside reality, your prospect isn't going to be able to figure out your <u>true</u> inside reality based on your marketing.

You simply appear to be just another business that sells whatever it is that you sell. And don't say, *"Well, that's OK because I have a salesperson... and when they get in front of my prospects they'll be able to educate them and close the sale."*

Listen, that's a great theory, but I can flat guarantee that even your best salesperson is never going to close a prospect who doesn't know you exist and therefore never bothers to contact you in the first place. How can you close people who never contact you? Obviously you can't!

That's why your marketing MUST do the heavy lifting for you. Let your marketing deliver eager, qualified prospects to your sales funnel. But here's even worse news.

Competition today is fiercer now than it's ever been. How many competitors do you have right now in your business? Because that's how many choices your prospects have and that's how many additional businesses they have to sift through and filter through as they attempt to reach a buying decision.

And by the way, the internet has only made the problem worse! Have you noticed lately that everyone's going bonkers for online marketing? SEO, pay-per-click, Facebook, social marketing! And rightfully so. Most prospects are so busy these days that most of them start their buying process by researching online.

But here's the sad reality for businesses that are advertising online. They spend a ton of their time and a ton of their effort and money... just to get prospects to their website.

And guess what their prospects see when they get there? The

same old, lame junk like "service, quality and dependability" that they saw in their lame brochure before the Internet was invented as well as the same lame junk that all their competitors have on their websites.

These businesses then curse their high bounce rate... and they try to figure out how to get better-qualified traffic to visit their site. The reality is that they're probably already getting enough qualified traffic to their site... but they fail to realize that it's their lame website that's not converting their prospects that's the real problem.

Everyone looks at the Internet as the end-all-be-all to all of their marketing problems.

But the reality is that the Internet is just another medium to screw up your marketing with bland messages that do nothing to facilitate the decision-making process of your prospects. Yes... the Internet is an important tool in your marketing arsenal. But you need to have a great website... and that means you better fix your strategic messaging that I've been talking about or you're going to fail.

There's an old saying that goes like this: if you want to know why Jane Doe buys what Jane Doe buys, you've got to see the world through Jane Doe's eyes.

But the problem is that, while most businesses are very good at knowing what Jane Doe wants, because they aren't communications experts, they don't have the ability to communicate through their advertising and marketing their inside reality to the outside world. They can't lead their prospects to say, *"I would be an idiot to do business with anyone other than you... at anytime, anywhere or at any price."*

It's been my experience that most businesses could stand some improvement in both their inside reality and their outside perception. But for some reason, they struggle the most with their outside perception. In other words, they've got great businesses... most of them offer exceptional value they have a good inside reality.

But with all the competition that exists, they have a major problem differentiating themselves from the rest of their marketplace. They're simply not getting the value of their business across to those on the outside looking in.

What about you? What's your outside perception? Go grab your marketing, look at your ads, take a look at your website. Is it instantly obvious, specifically and quantifiably, what makes you better and unique and different?

Do you show your prospects how to judge your industry, what factors they need to consider when deciding what to buy, and how you provide greater value than any of your competitors? You'll realize as these concepts start to sink in that the crux of most marketing problems -- including yours -- can be wrapped up in this one simple statement.

Most businesses outside perception is not an accurate reflection of their inside reality. So I'm going to show you why this is happening... and what you can do to fix this for your business... forever! **I told you at the beginning of this chapter that everything you know about generating leads and growing your business is wrong.**

Let me clarify what that statement means based on what we've discussed so far. Everything you currently know about marketing does <u>not</u> effectively allow you to accurately and succinctly portray your inside reality to the outside world.

The Truth!

It's Not Your Fault

"If you can't find a valid model for success in your category, then look at what everyone else is doing and do the opposite"

\-   Earl Nightingale

This is a product of decades of being conditioned to do marketing the WRONG way.

In the very early days of advertising, I'm talking the late 1800s and early 1900s; much of the advertising that existed back then was comparative in nature. Ads wouldn't just say, *"Hey, we're better!"* They'd say, *"We're better... and here's exactly why... based on this and that."*

On average, they did a pretty good job of building a case and helping prospective buyers understand the important issues in regards to their particular product or service. The result was that the outside perception was generally a pretty good reflection of the company's inside reality.

Then the most significant event in the history of marketing and advertising occurred in 1945:   Television was commercially introduced for the first time.

Up until then, total national distribution of an advertising message was extremely limited to radio; print advertising in a few magazines... and maybe a big name catalog. But with the introduction of TV, large advertisers could buy a TV commercial and reach just about every living person in the country for €4,000 a minute, usually sold in one or two minute blocks. What a bargain, even in 1950's money!

But back then there were only three channels, so demand quickly outstripped the supply of commercials, and prices shot through the roof. In response to the rising cost, the length of commercials shrank down from two minutes to 30 seconds.

This meant that advertisers had less time to educate us to the important and relevant issues... and build a case as to why they were different or better or unique.

So instead of attempting to use shorter ads that highlighted their comparative benefits, advertisers changed tactics and started using slogans.

That change made it harder and harder for the company's outside perception to accurately reflect its inside reality.

But remember that marketing's first job is simply to get the prospect's attention. Even running just 30 second ads, getting attention was still not a problem for these advertisers. But then what? That's right: after you grab the prospect's attention, you must next facilitate their decision-making process.

Companies and their ad agencies found that this was a lot harder to do in only 30 seconds, but they also found out that they didn't really need to do it, because the number of real competitors -- that is, the number of competitors that could actually afford to advertise on TV and run ads against their ads -- was wonderfully few.

They could spend a ton of money running 30 second ads and win by default. Now, if there happened to be two or three major competitors jockeying for the same prospects like Pepsi and Coke that was fine, because there was plenty of business to divide two or three ways.

The bottom line is that a company's inside reality and outside perception didn't really have to match up. The lack of a substantial number of choices eliminated this necessity. So the focus for all marketing and advertising shifted to simply getting the prospect's attention.

That's when advertising lost its penchant for selling and instead, shifted its focus to creativity. The idea now was to get in the consumer's brain with something creative that would stimulate them and cause them to recall the product later on when they needed it. That's when slogans became the de facto marketing standard that is still in use today.

This new <u>creative</u> approach took over advertising as we know it and it soon began to filter into all other advertising media, including radio, Google Adwords, newspaper, magazines, billboards, golden pages, websites you name it.

Once this new <u>creative</u> message was in place, the big companies opened up their checkbooks, spent lots of money, and basically gave people no other option but to remember their message. After hearing "things go better with Coke" for the 8,000th time you're going to remember it whether you want to or not.

We call this "C and R advertising," C for creativity and R for repetition. Create an ad that is unusual, weird, shocking, funny emotional and so on spend a billion Euros running that ad about a million times and then haul your dough down to the bank.

We call this the era of the brand-builders and in the 1950s, 60s, and even into the 70s, it was a no-brainer formula for market dominance for the companies with the financial wherewithal to pull this off. And that's when it happened!

Ad agencies started running this formula for all of their other clients, even the ones that were smaller and didn't have deep pockets.

Business schools started teaching marketing and advertising based on these methods that were being successfully implemented by the largest companies in the world, and churning out graduates who only knew one way to do marketing.

Brand-builder marketing and advertising became the de facto standard for how you do it. And after a few years, no one even questioned the formula. Which brings us to the crux of the problem.

All of us alive today, with no exceptions -- grew up in an era where almost all of the advertising you've ever seen or heard is a product of the era of the brand-builders. Over time, we've all become conditioned as to what constitutes a good advertisement.

We learned the fundamental pattern for what to put into a commercial. We learned about slogans and jingles and being funny.

We learned that, in marketing and advertising, the outside perception no longer has to reflect the inside reality.

And as a result of this new breed of advertising... jargon has now started to dominate ALL marketing and advertising. Think of jargon as words or phrases that are drearily commonplace and predictable... that lack power to evoke interest through overuse or repetition... and that are nevertheless stated as if they were original or significant. In advertising, you see and hear jargon all the time.

Since businesses only have 30 seconds to try to convey what makes them special, they lump everything into jargon such as "largest selection," "most professional," "lowest prices," "highest quality," "best service," "fastest," "most convenient," "largest in the country," "more honest," "we're the experts," "we specialize," "works harder," "gets the job done right the first time," and "been in business for 4,000 years."

Now listen, I'm not saying that you shouldn't be those kinds of things.

Those actually make up the foundation you want to use to build your inside reality on. But consider this. If my marketing says that I offer high quality and great service, isn't that drearily commonplace and predictable?

Doesn't it lack power to evoke interest through overuse or repetition?

Isn't it nevertheless stated as though it were original and significant?

Does my inside reality, what really makes me good at what I do -- does that really shine through?

Can you tell specifically what makes me valuable to the marketplace when I say "highest quality" or "best service"?

See, you simply can't describe, demonstrate, exhibit, reveal, or display your inside reality using jargon. It's impossible!

And unfortunately, the end result is an outside perception that you're no different than anyone else. There's absolutely no distinction, no separation, and no differentiation. None. You just flat-out can't make your inside reality and outside perception match up when you use jargon like this.

In fact, let me give you several ways you can easily and quickly evaluate your own marketing to see if you're getting caught up in the jargon trap. Jargon evaluation #1 is what we call, *"Well, I would hope so."*

When you make a claim, don't think about it in terms of the words coming out of your mouth. Think about it in terms of the words entering your prospect's ears. This will enable you to realize just how absurd most jargon sounds. Look at the messaging in your marketing, and then ask yourself if the prospect's immediate response might be, *"Well, I would hope so."* Let me give you an example.

I recently saw a TV ad for a window company. Throughout the ad they continuously emphasized the fact that their work was of the highest quality... it was fairly priced and they guaranteed 100% satisfaction.

Well, I would hope so. Would you hire ANY window company who didn't provide all of those as a standard part of their service? Of course not. This is ALL jargon... drearily commonplace... lacks power to evoke interest through overuse or repetition.

How about this one from a consulting company: *"Our training leads to change. We increase the productivity, performance, and profit of your company."* Well I would hope so!

Does anyone hire a consultant for any other reason than to do those things? Most ads today are nothing more than a jargon-fest. Does this jargon tell you anything about these companies inside reality? What else would you expect them to say? Everyone's always going to say wonderful things about their company if they can get away with it.

The problem is that if your company has an exceptional inside reality... and you're using the same jargon as everyone else... then the outside perception is that you're all the same.

And that's when prospects default to the company offering the lowest price. Price now becomes the only determining factor. When you use this simple evaluation, just ask yourself openly and honestly WHY anyone would choose you over your competition? Then evaluate your answer against the *"well, I would hope so"* evaluation.

And finally, check out all of your advertising and marketing materials, including your website. Do they pass the "well, I would hope so" evaluation, or are they ALL chock full of jargon? If they fail, then you need to make changes.

Let me provide you with a second evaluation technique. It's called *"Who else can say that?"*

This is similar to the first evaluation technique... and it's also a product of the era of the brand-builders. Pay very close attention to this one.

Stop thinking in terms of *"Who else can do what you do?"* Instead, think in terms of *"Who else can say what you say?"*

Because the answer, unfortunately, is usually "anybody and everybody can say what you say."

I know of a kitchen remodeler that ran by far the most impressive remodeling company in his community. Every member of his crew had at least 15 years of remodeling experience... they were all certified sub-contactors... they had won multiple industry awards... they were the only kitchen remodeling company that provided not only a full satisfaction guarantee, but also a 10 year material and labor warranty on everything they did.

They left the jobsite every night cleaner than when they first arrived. They also guaranteed they could remodel any kitchen in no more than 5 days... half the time of their competitors. This of course, meant far less disruption and inconvenience to the homeowner.

In short, their inside reality was literally second-to-none. But they had a huge marketing problem. Their marketing looked virtually identical to all of their far less-worthy competitors.

Their marketing said things like: "certified sub-contractors," "guaranteed satisfaction," and then a long laundry list of the work they performed, such as new cabinets installed...

complete kitchen remodeling and so on. Oh... and get this... they accept Visa and Master Card!

Well I would hope so!

But then ask this question: Who else can say that?

When the owner of this remodeling company was asked that very question... he got really defensive. He said, *"There's no other remodeler that can begin to match the work we do! Our sub-contractors are far-and-away the best there is! No one -- and I mean no one -- can say what we say!"*

Understandably, this contractor was extremely passionate and protective when it came to the superior company he had worked so long and hard to develop over the years.

So finally, to try to get the point across to him, he was asked to pull up the websites of his five biggest competitors and see what all of them were saying on their home page.

Let's just say that his jaw hung open for about two minutes straight before he finally pointed at the screen and said, "Oh my gosh... look at this other company's website. I know this guy. He's terrible.

But his site says the exact same thing as mine. In fact, I think he copied my site word-for-word!" He looked at the other remodelers and saw that all of their websites were virtually identical to his.

So remember... it's not who can do what you do. It's *"who can say what you say?"*

And if you're marketing is full of jargon, and then sadly that answer is all of your competitors can. Let me give you one final jargon detection evaluation. It's called the scratch-out write-in test. Take a look at your brochure... advertisement or website. Now, scratch out your name and write in your competitor's name. That's it.

If the marketing is still valid, if the website still conveys the same basic message, if there wouldn't need to be any additional changes... then guess what?

You just failed this test.

This evaluation can be very revealing. Most businesses discover that they run fairly high on the jargon meter. You may find that your inside reality, excellent as it may be, is nowhere to be found in your marketing messaging.

It's all but lost in a sea of jargon and completely invisible to your prospects. Is this making sense to you?

Is it evident that this might be a problem for you now... and a tremendous competitive advantage if you could figure out how to fix this for your own business?

So let me show you how to fix this.

An equation that generates leads at will...

"Wonder what your customer really wants? Ask. Don't tell."

- Lisa Stone

First I'm going to explain how you can follow a very simple process I call the marketing equation and when you do you will eliminate jargon forever.

I'm going to show you how to become a communications powerhouse make your outside perception become an excellent reflection of your inside reality and finally begin to get the results from your marketing that you should be getting.

Once you understand the marketing equation I'm going to dive in deeper into this equation and give you a step by step plan for implementing it into your own business.

The marketing equation has four main components. Let me start with a brief introduction, and then I'll go into more detail.

The first component of the marketing equation is called **Interrupt.** This is simply the process of getting qualified prospects to pay attention to your marketing.

This is often accomplished by affecting the prospect emotionally. Sounds simple enough doesn't it? Unfortunately, it's a lot more difficult to pull this off in real life unless you understand what you're about to learn here.

The second component is **engage**. Once the prospect is interrupted, it's critical to give the reader the promise that information is forthcoming that will help the prospect make the best decision possible or, in other words, facilitate their decision-making process. This is also best accomplished on an emotional level.

The third component is **educate**. Once you've interrupted and engaged the prospect, you have to give them information that allows them to <u>logically</u> understand how and why you solved that emotional problem.

This is accomplished by giving detailed, quantifiable, specific, inside-reality-revealing information. This turns the corner from an emotional sell -- remember you interrupted and engaged them based on emotional hot buttons -- to a logical sell. This is easy to do if you just follow this marketing equation.

And the fourth and final component of the marketing equation is the **offer**. Now the prospect has been interrupted based on problems that are important to them emotionally engaged by the promise of a solution to that emotional problem and they've examined the educational information that makes your solution to that emotional problem real and believable.

So the last step is for you to give that prospect a low or better yet no risk way for them to take the next step in the sales process. This can be accomplished by offering a free marketing tool -- such as a report, brochure, seminar, audio, video, or something similar -- that educates them even more so the prospect feels in complete control of the decision-making process.

This marketing equation follows the formula for what marketing is supposed to do in the first place. In fact, at this point, you can simply say that marketing's job is to interrupt, engage, educate, and offer.

Remember earlier I discussed that if you want to know why Jane Doe buys what Jane Doe buys; you've got to see the world through Jane Doe's eyes, right? Well, I would submit to you that if you want to know what Jane Doe sees, you'd better first understand how Jane Doe's brain works how it processes information and makes decisions.

To understand this process, there are three major concepts that I need to teach you.

These are three concepts that very few in the world of marketing understands but three concepts that will make all the difference in the world in your marketing's effectiveness and, more importantly, in your company's profitability.

The three things you need to know about Jane Doe's brain are downtime, uptime, and the reticular activation system also known as the reticular activator.

Let's begin by discussing that first concept called downtime.

Simply put, this is the hypnotic state of running automatic patterns that allows your brain to perform habitual tasks without any conscious thought.

You do this all the time. For instance, have you ever driven to work and when you got there you don't remember making the trip? That's downtime.

This occurs because driving to work is a habitual pattern that you run so frequently that you don't have to consciously think about it.

Have you ever stepped out of the shower and couldn't remember if you shampooed your hair or not? Your brain performs all of these daily routine functions with no conscious thought.

Now, here's what downtime means in marketing terms: People see and hear ads with their eyes and ears, but they don't notice them on a conscious level.

If you open a newspaper, you'll be looking at maybe 70% ads

and only 30% bonafide news articles; but because the ads are only seen on a downtime level, 9.9 times out of 10 you won't consciously notice them at all.

All you consciously see is the news, which is what you were there for in the first place.

The second concept is what's known as uptime.

This is the brain's state of alertness or active engagement. It's like when you're driving on the freeway in a heavy thunderstorm your hands firmly gripped on the wheel at the ten and two o'clock positions and your pupils are as big as saucers.

You're sensitive and responsive to everything around you. You're in uptime when you're watching a horror movie and you hear the music building to a crescendo in anticipation of something scary happening! You can think of uptime as your brain going on alert mode.

 But here's what uptime means when it comes to your marketing. When your prospect is in uptime mode... they consciously notice your ad or marketing piece and they're open to your suggestions and solutions.

Something captures their attention and compels them to keep paying attention.

The key to marketing is to get your prospect out of downtime and into uptime.

We want to shake them out of their natural subconscious haze, where they never see your ad or marketing piece, and into uptime, where they are fully conscious and aware of what you're trying to communicate to them.

Once you understand how to do this you'll have the ability to make a fortune with your marketing.

But to completely grasp this model, you've got to learn the third major concept about how Jane Doe's brain works, which is called the reticular activator.

The reticular activator is the part of your brain that's on the lookout 24 hours a day, 7 days a week even when you're asleep. It constantly scans the environment looking for things that fall into any of these three categories: things that are familiar, things that are unusual, and things that are problematic.

When the brain detects any of these three categories on a subconscious level, it sends a message over to the conscious side of the brain and says, "Hey! Wake up! There's something here you need to pay attention to."

And by the way whatever those familiar, unusual, or problematic things are we call them activators.

In short, your brain on a subconscious level is constantly on the lookout for activators.

It's searching for things that are familiar things that are unusual... or things that are problematic. In other words things that demand a conscious response.

Whenever it finds one, it pokes your conscious brain and snaps it out of downtime sleep mode and into uptime alert mode.

Let me give you an example of the raw power of your own reticular activator and please don't get mad at me for what I'm about to do to you.

But I'm going to permanently embed this example directly into your reticular activation system and I GUARANTEE that you will remember this for the remainder of your life on this planet.

The Truth!

Seriously. Here we go.

I'm certain that at some point over your lifetime you have glimpsed a FedEx truck making its deliveries. FedEx has been in business since June 18th, 1971.

That's a lot of years those trucks have been driving around town. So let me ask you a question.

How many times have you seen those FedEx trucks?

Over the 40 plus years they have been in business... I would wager to say you have seen their trucks a minimum of 1,000 times. So here's question number two.

Have you <u>ever</u> seen the hidden message within the FedEx logo?

Yes... that's a serious question. Did you know that there is a hidden message within every FedEx logo? If you're saying right now that's impossible you've seen that logo thousands of times and you certainly would have noticed a message in there at some point in time then join the crowd. 99% of the population has NEVER seen that hidden message.

Ready for me to tell you where it is?

Next time you see a FedEx logo, look between the E and X in FedEx.

You will see an arrow pointing to the right. It's as plain as day... and yet very few people have ever detected it over all these years.

And guess what that logo was specifically designed that way from the start it isn't just something that happened by coincidence when the designer created it. Almost NO ONE sees it. But guess what?

FedEx

Express

YOU will now see it... EVERY single time you look at that logo. Why?

Because now that I have drawn your attention to it coupled with the fact you had NO idea it was there before the next time you see that arrow your brain will perceive it to be unusual and that automatically triggers your reticular activator.

Remember things that are familiar, unusual or problematic poke your brain and make it pay attention through your reticular activator.

But guess what is going to happen next?

Now that you know that arrow is there, EVERY time you see that FedEx logo, your brain will immediately seek out that arrow.

And as you observe it over and over, the arrow will move from being unusual to being familiar. And in both of those cases, guess what else happens.

You will only notice the arrow for a second or two because your brain activates when it sees it moving you from downtime into uptime but since the arrow isn't really relevant or important to you, your brain quickly reverts to downtime.

The Truth!

This Changes Everything...

"Ideas are easy. Implementation is hard."

- Guy Kawasaki

So what does all this have to do with marketing then? The short answer is everything. Understanding what wakes people up so they pay attention is what's going to get our marketing message past the "interrupt" stage and onto the "engage" stage.

And when we engage your prospect, we've just increased our chances of selling to the people you're trying to engage by one thousand percent!

This is going to solve the problem that every other marketer hasn't been able to figure out, which is not just getting them interrupted but also getting them engaged not just finding any old activator but finding the right activator.

Any idiot can simply interrupt people -- in fact, that's actually VERY easy to do.

The so-called marketing gurus over in the big corporate advertising agencies do it all the time. Those guys and gals prefer to use activators that are based on things that are familiar and unusual because they're the easiest to pull off.

Have you ever noticed how many different kinds of animals you see in advertising?

That's because animals are familiar and likable, and the idea is that those animals will interrupt you by poking your conscious brain when they're detected by your reticular activator. Aflac has the duck, Compare the Market has the meerkat and Coke has its polar bears. You constantly see dancing elephants, talking dogs and finicky cats.

All of these animals have good interim value based on their familiarity. That's also the major reason that big advertisers use celebrities: familiarity.

And what about activators based on unusual things? Well, that's what creativity is all about.

Creativity's main purpose in advertising is to dream up something so weird, so strange, so shocking, and so unusual that it'll snap you out of downtime and into uptime, otherwise known as "interrupt."

But here's the key, here's what no one else seems to understand and what just may be the most important thing you'll learn in this book.

Once the brain is activated, once it's been broken out of downtime and into uptime alert mode, it wants to be engaged. So it immediately and subconsciously searches for additional, clarifying information.

The brain wants to know, *"Hey! What's this all about? How does this affect me? Do I need to do anything about this?"* Literally on a subconscious level, the brain goes on a fact-finding mission.

The bottom line is the brain wants to know, "How is this important and relevant to me? Should I allocate any conscious bandwidth to this?"

So it searches for additional facts. If it finds them, it'll become engaged. If not, it will quickly revert back into downtime.

We call these important, relevant issues "hot buttons." If you're a golf fan and your reticular activator detects that Tiger Woods is on the television, it notices that on a conscious level because

Tiger Woods is familiar. He's an activator.

Then your brain immediately asks, "Hey, what's Tiger Woods doing driving a Buick? Is there anything here that's relevant or important to me?" Or in other words, is this a hot button issue for me at this point in my life?

What typically happens is your brain determines that Buick is not important or relevant to you, it doesn't do anything to solve any of your problems and therefore it's not a hot button. And so your brain immediately reverts back into downtime. Let me be crystal clear here.

An activator is something that snaps a person from downtime to uptime and it's based on something that's familiar, unusual, or problematic. But an activator can also be classified as a hot button if -- and only if -- it's based on something that's important and relevant to your prospect.

Your best bet to successfully interrupt and engage your target market is to identify problems, frustrations, uncertainties, and annoyances your prospects have and then address them in your marketing.

Their pain in most cases is their hot button. And please don't think this is some form of manipulation.

All we're doing here is tapping into the problems that your prospects already have. We're NOT trying to manufacture a crisis for them. We're merely poking their problems and pointing out those problems so that their reticular activator notices and brings us onto their active radar screen.

Now, here's the key point in all of this, and one that none of the big ad agencies understand, but one that you need to know in order to make this all work for you.

The activators that are used to interrupt the prospect <u>must</u> be based on a relevant hot button. If not, the prospect will <u>momentarily</u> be interrupted but will quickly revert from uptime back into downtime. This is what we call "false uptime."

Have you ever heard someone call out your name in a crowded room? That IMMEDIATELY interrupts you because your name is familiar.

But when you turn around to see who it was that was calling you, you realize, *"Oops, they were actually calling out to someone else with my name."*

Your name is an activator but because in that situation your name wasn't important or relevant to you, it didn't engage you. You quickly reverted right back to downtime. That's what we call false uptime.

Remember what I just said about the FedEx logo?

Now that you know the arrow is there, EVERY time you see it your brain will immediately seek it out because it's unusual. But the more often you see it, that arrow shifts from being unusual to being familiar.

Then you will only notice it for a second or two and then your brain quickly reverts back into downtime because the arrow isn't relevant or important to you. This happens in marketing and advertising all the time. Most marketing interrupts, but it doesn't engage.

Just like in the Unites States with Tiger Woods and Buick: He's famous, and you like golf, so it captures your attention; it interrupts you. But when you find out that it's not based on anything that's important to you, when there's nothing relevant, nothing that solves some problem that you have, you quickly revert to downtime.

The Truth!

This is one of the things that almost no one understands and one of the main reasons everything you've ever learned about marketing is wrong.

You've been conditioned to believe that, as long as you've interrupted the prospect, that's it! That's good enough! The job is done.

But you have to realize that if you only interrupt the prospect, that's only one fourth of the marketing equation. You've got to include all four components: interrupt, engage, educate, and offer to get the maximum results from your marketing and advertising.

Now, when it comes to actually writing the marketing, we typically like to portray the hot buttons in the form of headlines.

The headline is the first opportunity you have to interrupt Jane Doe. You've got maybe one to three seconds max to interrupt the prospect, so you'd better make sure that the headline has activators in it and that those activators are based on things that are important and relevant to that prospect.

Remember, hot buttons; words and phrases that describe problems or frustrations that the prospect is feeling so that their reticular activator latches onto them and snaps them into uptime. In print advertising, magazines, newspapers, golden pages, and so forth, the form of the headline is obvious. In radio, the headline is the first sentence they hear.

On Google Adwords, it's the first bit of text they read. On television it's the first thing they see and hear. In brochures, business cards, other marketing collateral and your company website, it's the first thing they see.

How to dominating your marketplace

"The only thing worse than starting something and failing... is not starting something."

- Seth Godin

Now that I covered the basic of the marketing equation, it's time to dive deeper into it. This will help you understand the fundamentals that make up "competition-crushing" marketing.

The business owner who understands how to create messages, ads and marketing collateral that follows a persuasion format can literally gain the ability to dominate their market. Before we cover that though, I want to introduce you to what's called "persuasion marketing".

Persuasion Marketing is organizing the buying and selling processes to present compelling information that persuades your prospects to take a specific action. All marketing should inform and persuade your prospects, address the wants and needs of prospects that they continue to move through their various decision-making stages within your sales and marketing process.

The Problem with "Experts"
So called marketing "experts" use tips, tricks, tools, and gimmicks and the problem with this is:

- Prospects have "wised-up" to the trickery
- They have become jaded, skeptical and distrustful

Smart business owners must start thinking outside the box and you must adopt persuasion marketing to help you do this.

Persuasion can be described as: Logical discussion + good data + logical facts = persuasion. From this you could break the persuasion process down to three main steps:

1. Present your proposition clearly, and with conviction
2. Present your supporting data, with the right facts, logic and information
3. Structure your "deals" and move on to the close

This may look all well on paper but following this process is one surefire way to fail at persuasion. This process misses one key ingredient – human nature! Our brains requires 300 percent more effort—measured in calories burned—for heavy thinking compared with "mental cruising".

Instead start thinking in terms of "Hot buttons" – which are our automatic self-guidance systems. They help us make easy, non-analytical, yet correct decisions. Master persuasion marketing and you will attract more clients... attract them with greater frequency at a lower cost... and with total and complete confidence and certainty.

Seven Fundamentals to Understanding Human Behaviour

Fundamental #1 – Everyone wants the "best deal"

By best deal, this doesn't mean getting the lowest price. When I refer to best deal, I'm referring to getting the most VALUE. Think of it this way, people will happily pay twice the price (compared to another product or service) if they perceive four times the value.

Fundamental #2 – Marketing to the Negative

A big concept I talked about in my first book Your Elephant's Under Threat (details at the end of this book) is something I originally learned from Tony Robbins. It's the pleasure pain theory. We will do anything to avoid pain... but little to gain pleasure. People make decisions to either avoid pain or gain pleasure and often times will do more to avoid pain than they will to gain pleasure. In terms of marketing your business you can put this to your advantage by positioning your product or service as the solution to their "hot button" issues.

Fundamental #3 – Prospects buy based on emotion

Human beings make buying decisions based on emotion. We only use logic to justify our purchases. Your prospects want to avoid pain, and that resonates with them emotionally.

You can capitalize on this by taking advantage of fundamental #2 and marketing to the negative and make your marketing emotionally compelling. Doing so will hit your prospects squarely in their hot buttons, and you automatically make an emotional connection bonding them to you in a way your competitors won't because chances are your competitors are marketing using boring, ineffective platitudes like I discussed earlier in this book.

Fundamental #4 – Make your business "unique"

You must be able to create and define a market dominating position that separates yourself from your competitors. My mentor, Dan Kennedy has a famous question that at the very least you should answer when it comes to creating your market dominating position.

"Why should I your prospective customer, choose to do business with you versus any and every other category available to me, including doing nothing at all."

The best way to make your business unique is to create a "niche" market for your business. Stop trying to be everything to everyone. When you select a niche market, you instantly become "unique". Some examples of niche markets are as follows:

- Web design exclusively for personal trainers.
- Fitness training for busy mums over 40.
- Marketing consulting for coaches and trainers.

Fundamental #5 – Create "extraordinary value"

Your prospects shop price because they're forced to and often times if you're competing on price it's because you have not engineered your business or created enough value to differentiate yourself from your competitors. Remember fundamental #1, prospects want the best "value" for the price they pay. One way to start portraying value in your business is stop thinking in terms of the features of what you offer but instead think in terms of the benefits of what you offer. Prospects want to know how they will benefit from what you sell.

One of my many favourite sources of marketing inspiration and wizardry is the infamous Gary Halbert. The price of print and self proclaimed 'greatest copywriter that ever lived' had a great exercise he used to do himself and one he encouraged all business owners to do is the features/benefits exercise. Sadly, few business owners take the time to actually complete this task but you won't make that mistake will you? Of course you won't.

Features vs. benefits:
1. Write down all of you current product and service offerings.
2. Write down every feature of your products and/or services.
3. Translate these features directly into the benefits your clients or customers receive from these features.

For e.g. a new TV might have a surround sound as a feature but the benefit is that you will feel as if you're actually in the cinema when watching. Always, be thinking in terms of benefits.

Fundamental #6 – Communicate your uniqueness and extraordinary value

Once you know your target market you need to create a highly targeted, laser-focused message. This again is direct response marketing 101, message to market match. You'd be surprised the amount of so called marketing 'experts' I've met and spoken with hadn't the first iota about message to market match. One of these 'experts' had even the audacity to write a book on marketing! The world we live in.

Your message must tell them you have exactly what they want. It will serve as your elevator pitch, whether you're portraying that message, in person, over the phone, online through email, a webinar or social media.

By the way if you want the foremost information, resources and training on the message, market and media match triangle then look no further than GKIC (www.GKIC.ie). By way of an almost free trial you can join *the place for prosperity*. It's almost free in that all you pay is the meager shipping and handling fee to send you some of the best marketing information on the planet today. As a GKIC certified business advisor I'm undoubtedly biased but there's a reason why my mentor Dan Kennedy is called 'the millionaire maker'. Visit www.GKIC.ie/truth for full details.

Fundamental #7 – Prospect buy what they want... not what they need

Remember, needs are based on logic, "wants" are based on emotion. When you create marketing messages based on emotion, you will absolutely dominate your competition

How do you create persuasive marketing?

It's quite simple. Marketing is a science and there's a simple equation that always produces the right result. That equation is known as the "Marketing Equation.

If you take nothing away from this short and powerful book, let it be this; there are 3 things that marketing MUST do.

1. Marketing MUST grab the reader's attention

2. It MUST facilitate the prospect's information gathering & decision making process

3. It MUST provide a specific, low risk, easy to take action that helps them make a good decision

Why are these 3 steps so important?

Remember, the four basic components of the marketing equation are: Interrupt, Engage, Educate and Offer. This equation appeals to consumers' emotional & social wants & needs. It focuses your message to impact your prospect's mind. Nowadays more so than ever your prospects are suffocating in marketing messages.

Think about it, how many emails do you get a day with the latest whiz-bang launch, how many solicitations do you get every day from some super company promising the world? Your inbox is full, your newsfeed is full of sponsored posts, and the papers are full of advertising, its everywhere.

What happens is your prospects filter most messages out of their conscious thought unless one happens to hit them squarely on their hot button.

First, all marketing must grab the prospect's attention
> if it doesn't, it's worthless… they'll never read, watch or listen to the rest of your ad
> the best way to get attention is to have a great headline

Second, every prospect is always looking for the best deal
> in order to know if something is the best deal, they must have decision making information
> your marketing MUST help the prospect gather information that aids them in their decision making process
> develop a client profile and map out your prospects decision making process

Third, your marketing must contain a low, or no risk offer to further facilitate the prospects decision making process
> give them a compelling & safe way to take the next step
> it may be to pick up the phone to make an appointment, order a free trial, or visit a retail location
> you want a concrete action step that gets your prospect actively involved with your business

These three principles must always be present if your marketing is going to be effective. How do you ensure you follow these principles? *By following the marketing equation.*

Next, we're going to break down the equation into its four component pieces and examine them individually before tying everything together with an exercise for you to complete. Yes, you have to take action on this if you want to start getting results.
The Marketing Equation…

The Truth!

- Interrupt
- Engage
- Educate
- Offer

We'll begin with Interrupt...

Step 1: Interrupt

"Fail often so you can succeed sooner."

- Tom Kelley

You must interrupt your prospects so that they'll notice and pay attention to your message. This is done with an attention-grabbing headline. STOP putting the name of your business as well as your picture at the top of your ad or website. Prospects ONLY care about themselves. The headline must resonate with the hot button issues faced by that specific prospect in that specific niche market.

Let's look at some examples. Please, take these examples and look at them from the point of view of adapting the principles. Don't dismiss them because you're not in that specific business or you run an online business. The principles work no matter what type of business you run.

The Bad:

1.   Child Psychologist...

"Parenting Advice & Resources From Dr. John Smith"

Would this hit your "hot button" if you were dealing with a screaming child? Of course not!

The Good:

Child Psychologist...

"Are You Sick And Tired Of The Yelling, Screaming & Belligerent Attitude Of Your Child?"

Now would this hit your "emotional hot button?" A Euro gets ten, this one will outperform the first by 10 to 1. Every marketing piece MUST start with a headline that must grab the prospect's attention in an emotionally compelling way. The headline serves a second crucial function. It immediately qualifies your target customer and disqualifies those prospects who aren't your target customer.

A well-written headline will only grab the attention of those prospects who genuinely want your product or service. You must have no qualms of disqualifying people with your marketing. After all, it's much too expensive to be attracting and targeting people into your business who you either wouldn't like working with or are not a good for your business.

Let's take a look at an example for a child care. Imagine a child care that specializes in children ages 3 months through 3 years old. The reason why I'm choosing this example is because I've have the privilege of mentoring a childcare, Montessori and afterschool business in my hometown in Galway.

Now imagine that other child cares have a staff-to-child ratio of about 10:1. Here after doing your research you find out that the target customer's hot button is that they want their child to receive personal, undivided attention and supervision from the child care staff. They will immediately respond to marketing highlighting this issue. So what could you do if you were in the childcare business?

Well the first thing you could do is what Peter Drucker calls one of the most important aspects in your business (out of the two most important) – innovate. You could innovate your child care to offer a staff-to-child ratio of 5:1. Oh by the way, in case you don't know or hadn't guessed, the second most important aspect is marketing.

Once you had innovated your business you would then use hot

button & innovation for an attention-grabbing headline that you could use in any of your advertising collateral, be it a newspaper ad, a sales letter, your website, your business card, flyers, or brochures. Your headline needs to be in the largest font of whatever collateral you decide to use.

"Ever Feel Like Your Child Care Treats Your Child Like a Number Instead of a Little Person?"

Step 2: Engage

"A 'startup' is a company that is confused about – 1. What its product is. 2. Who its customers are. 3. How to make money."

- Dave McClure

Once you have interrupted your prospect with an emotionally triggered 'hot button' headline, next you must engage them and this is the job of the sub-headline. The sub-headline engages by persuasively promising to provide them with vital decision-making information that will solve their major problem, frustration, fear or concern. It builds on the impact of the headline and makes it intriguing

So right after my headline says...

Ever Feel Like Your Child Care Treats Your Child Like a Number Instead of a Little Person?

My sub-headline would say...

Here's How to Insure Your Child Gets Personal, Loving, Caring, One-on-One Attention at Child Care

Your sub-headline should be in the second-largest font. Place it directly below, or immediately after your headline. The headline and sub-headline work together to Interrupt and Engage your target customer by promising to provide them with vital, decision making information that will solve their major concern or frustration.

Here are some additional examples of the headline and sub-headline working in tandem. Note, for illustrative purposes, font size is not representative of true size.

Need To Sell Your Home Fast?

Eleven Steps Will Get You More Money & Sell Your Home In
Half The Time

One In Every Fourteen Homes Are Burglarized Every Day

Now You Can Completely Protect Your Family For Only 67
Cents Per Day

**Worried About Hiring A Plumber Who's More Interested In
Lining His Own Pockets Than Fixing Your Plumbing?**

Ask Any Plumber These Three Incriminating Questions And
See For Yourself

Writing headlines and sub-headlines takes practice, patience
and a great "swipe file". A swipe file is a collection of
previously used, tested and proven headlines and sub-
headlines that can be used as examples to help you get started
developing yours.

I have a dedicated swipe file that I use for myself and clients
and I highly recommend you starting building your own swipe
file. As a bonus with the training element to this book I include
my headline bank which contains more than 350 of the most
successful headlines ever. These are a great starting point for
anyone's swipe file. Details of how you can upgrade to this
training (if you have not already done so) is on page XX.

Step 3: Educate

"I try not to make any decisions that I'm not excited about."

- Jake Nickell

Once you have interrupted and engaged your prospects you must next educate them. You educate prospects with significant information about how your business delivers on the promise of the headline and sub-headline. This is the task of the body copy in your promotional materials.

Again this works for online in terms of squeeze pages, landing pages, or offline if it's promotional materials. Say for example if your marketing piece was for a lawyer, the headline and sub-headline would be your opening statement...

"Ladies and gentlemen of the jury, John Smith murdered Mike Jones, and I'll prove it by revealing four critical pieces of damaging evidence the prosecution doesn't want you to see"

Remember these important points, your body copy must convince prospects that you're the best. Telling them isn't enough—you have to prove it. In your body copy, emphasize benefits prospects want (refer to the Gary Halbert exercise a few pages back).

The biggest mistake is to focus on business's features. Here's a line you might want to remember, *Features tell, benefits sell*. Or to put into another way, businesses focused on features compete on price and businesses focused on benefits compete on value.

The body copy must inform your prospects about the extraordinary value you offer with crystal clarity. What if you don't currently offer extraordinary value? Then you need to innovate your business to create extraordinary value.

Just like Peter Drucker, one of the most amazing business leaders ever to grace us suggested, focusing on innovations is the key to marketing. In the child care example, lowering your daycares staff-to-child ratio is innovative.

How can you innovate your business?

Some key points to remember:

You want to focus on just that one hot button. Resist the temptation to throw in every bit of juicy information, and focus on only one hot button at a time. Give enough info to entice them to want to know more. Always highlight the benefits of your innovations. One ad, one hot button only – don't confuse them.

There's a specific syntax to use in the body copy. A syntax is a systematic orderly arrangement of information. A vast majority of prospects today merely skim ads. Develop body copy to facilitate their ability to scan your advertisements. Create short, benefit driven paragraphs that are always preceded with additional sub-headlines.

My mentor, Dan Kennedy calls this double readership path – which means that whether you read the whole thing or you just skim, you can get the full message.

Let's look at this in example format again. Sub-headlines must tell the basic story. They should be compelling enough to lead prospects directly to your offer, which is the call to action

Child care headline...

> *Ever Feel Like Your Child Care Treats Your Child*
> *Like a Number Instead of a Little Person?*

The Truth!

Followed by sub-headline...

Here's How to Insure Your Child Gets Personal, Loving, Caring, One-on-One Attention at Child Care

After the main sub-headline the body copy is broken down into five small paragraphs, with the following sub-headlines across the top of each paragraph:

Do You Know What The Teacher - Child Ratio Is At Your Child Care?

36%... That's The Percentage Of Kids Child Care Workers Know By Name

Here's How Other Child Cares Try To Disguise Their Lack Of Adequate Supervision

We Guarantee No More Than 5 Children To Every Staff Member

This Shocking Free Report Compares The Actual Teacher – Child Ratio At All 17 Area Child Care Facilities

So the syntax to follow when you create body copy for your marketing is...
- problem
- solution
- action

There are other variations of this that are used regularly and that I often use for myself. For example in an example I walk through a little later on in this book for company called SowEasyGrow.ie on I used the Star, Story, Solution formula that was made famous by Gary Halbert.

There's also the problem, agitate, solution or the problem, agitate, dig knife in their back and twist, solution. All of these work but for our simple example here I'm showing you problem, solution, action. Here we are using sub-headlines to describe the major points you want prospects to know based on the relevant hot button.

Step 4: Offer

"The astute business owner understands that the purpose of a sale is to generate a customer. The lousy business owner thinks that the purpose of a customer is to generate a sale. One lasts much longer and has much more fun than the other."

- Dan Kennedy

Always end your marketing message with a compelling offer. You'd be surprised how many advertisements I see day in, day out with absolutely no offer or a bland boring vanilla one. One terrible example of this is an ad for the car brand Infiniti.

I run a monthly business and marketing group (www.GKIC.ie for details) and one month, the topic was advertising mistakes to avoid. I used this ad example because, basically the ad consisted of a lake, some geese then switching to the Infiniti logo.

It was absolutely shocking and one of the worst ads in the world. Why, it meant absolutely nothing and there was no offer, no call to action, nothing. And the worst thing of all, the 'expert' marketing company that produced that ad was probably paid hundreds of thousands of Euros.

Your prospects won't take action unless you ask them to do so, and give them a good reason why they should. Offers have one purpose... get prospects to take action. Offers need to be a low- or better yet... no-risk way to lead your prospect to take the next step in your sales process. If you sell a low- or moderately-priced product or service, the next step might be to buy:

- An expensive item might require additional information
- An excellent way is to offer a free informational report

If your business requires educating your prospects on the benefits of doing business with you, your compelling offer should revolve around a free informational report.

Back to the childcare example – the offer here might be...

This Shocking Free Report Compares The Actual
Teacher – Child Ratio At All 17 Area Child Care Facilities

This free report should be available upon request and you could either (preferably both) physically mailed it to them or use a landing page to instantly download the report. When prospects call or go online to request the report, you should capture their contact information.

If they don't buy immediately, begin a "drip campaign". A drip campaign educates prospects on your innovations and the benefits those innovations provide to them. Educate them so they conclude they would be an absolute fool to do business with any other business but yours.

The "Marketing Equation" of Interrupt, Engage, Educate and Offer should be used in EVERY marketing piece you create. Keep prospects focused on what makes you unique. If your business isn't unique, and you can't afford to innovate, then use "preemptive advertising". Advertise something you do that no one is drawing attention to. If you're the first one to make a claim, you own that claim... even if it's a standard practice in your industry.

Note: Some differentiation on generating and converting leads...

When generating leads, educate prospects in the body copy of your marketing collateral - ads, brochures or direct mail. Your collateral should be specifically designed to get prospects to raise their hand and let you know they're interested in buying what you sell.

When converting leads, you should educate them in the body copy of your marketing collateral - free reports, drip campaigns, scripts. These are specifically designed to close the sale and convince the prospect to complete the transaction.

Remember persuasion marketing using the marketing equation is a process... NOT an event. There's more to marketing than "getting your name out there". If an ad agency starts peddling you advertising so you can get your name out there, run a mile.

You now know the process, and you have the marketing equation to guide you through it. If you act on this information, you should see a dramatic increase in the number of leads you begin to generate... the number of clients you begin to attract... and the amount of money you see accumulating on your bottom line.

To help you along with this I've created some questions for you to answer along each stage of creating your marketing collateral using the marketing equation. Also, there's some more in depth video training that I have waiting for you in the members area at www.Wrong.ie so if you are reading a physical copy of this book and would like to become a member please visit our members area for access.

How do you stack up against the marketing equation?

"Words calculated to catch everyone may catch no one."

- Adlai Stevenson

Take out your latest advertising pieces whether it's your website, pages on your website, your ads, brochures, business cards, scripts and run them through these questions. For simplicity purposes and to ensure you get best results, the correct answers are capitalized.

Interrupt Questions:

1. Do you have a headline? YES/no
2. Is your company name or a play on words at the top of your marketing piece? yes/NO
3. If a headline exists, does it hit upon the hot button? YES/no
4. Is your headline powerfully worded and hits the HOT BUTTON passionately. YES/no

Engage Questions:

1. Is there something under the headline to make the reader want to keep reading? YES/no
2. Is the sub headline related to the internal conversation going on in your prospects mind? YES/no
3. Could the reader tell that they're will be decision making info ahead? YES/no
4. Are you using a HOT BUTTON based sub headline? YES/no
5. Will the reader be engaged by the sub headline and make them quickly want to scan ahead? YES/no

Educate Questions:

1. Are you educating your prospects and facilitating their decision making process? YES/no
2. Are you listing features instead of benefits? yes/NO
3. Are you building a good case for your offer? YES/no
4. Will your prospects begin to think they've fallen upon the exact solution to their problems? YES/no

Offer Questions:

1. Is there an offer? YES/no
2. Is it clear and specific to the prospects hot button? YES/no
3. Is it either a low barrier entry offer or an informational offer? YES/no
4. Is there a specific offer box or an associated landing page? YES/no
5. Is there a data capture element to the offer? YES/no
6. Are there nurturing pieces in place? YES/no

Bonus Questions:

1. Is the basis structure of the marketing equation in place? YES/no
2. Are correct fonts/heading sizes used? YES/no
3. Is there double readership path at play? YES/no

John Mulry, MSc

Proof this Equation Works

"It's probably better to know a great deal about one, two or several things than a tiny bit about everything"

- Dan Kennedy

Let me give you two quick examples. I didn't want to use just any old standard overused examples, for example since I originally come from a personal training background (again, the full story on my background is available in my first book Your Elephant's Under Threat, available at www.JohnMulry.com/elephant) I'd usually go for examples from the fitness industry or from the coaching industry.

For our purposes here though, I've decided to go a little leftfield and prove to you that the marketing equation. The first example is for a childcare/crèche and the second is for a child psychologist who works with teenagers with behavioral problems.

When I asked some childcare providers why parents should choose them instead of the 17 other local childcares, they almost always give me the same boring answers: "high quality," "attention to detail," "we supervise our staff better," "we're honest," "we've taken care of more than 200 kids," and so on. Nothing but jargon.

Unfortunately, this exact same jargon shows up in boring, ineffective headlines.

For instance, when I looked at the marketing of various childcares they said things like this: safe, nurturing and creative environment, optimize your child's development, acclaimed by thousands of parents, accredited by industry professionals, a leader in early childhood care and education.

The Truth!

Those were all real headlines from real ads! Jargon and more jargon. But note this as well. These headlines ALL speak to the childcare not to the prospect.

You could place the word "we" in front of all of that jargon and it would fit perfectly.

WE optimize your child's development... WE'RE acclaimed by thousands of parents... WE'RE accredited by industry professionals.

Prospects don't care about the childcare. They care about themselves and their kids. None of those headlines address the problems or concerns of the parents, do they?

If you really want to interrupt John and Jane Doe, you've got to use much more powerful language than that to get them to respond on an emotional level.

How about this headline to effectively communicate the concept of a safe, nurturing and creative environment.

Ever Felt Like Your Childcare Treated Your Child Like A Number Instead Of A Little Person?

Or how about this one to convey being a leader in early childhood care and education:

Is Your Childcare's Idea Of Good Educational Curriculum Watching Doc McStuffins on TV?

Or this one:

Introducing A Childcare Centre That Doesn't Consider Chips and Nuggets To Be One Of The Four Major Food Groups.

All three of these headlines work in tandem with close-up pictures that work to reinforce this powerful and compelling messaging. That headline that said:

Ever Felt Like Your Childcare Treated Your Child Like A Number Instead Of A Little Person?

Now imagine next to that headline you see a 4 year old child sitting in the corner with his head buried in his hands crying.

Talk about powerful, emotional and compelling. Talk about interrupting. See how these headlines speak to the issues of the prospect instead of the childcare?

See how they reflect a fanatical attention to detail that is the foundation of this childcare's inside reality? Of course you do, because it's obvious.

Now, what about the child psychologist who works with teenagers with behavioral problems?

Most of these types of professionals say things like: we offer parenting advice and resources, we can help get your teenager under control, learn the secrets of well-behaved teenagers.

If I was a parent with an out-of-control teenager, why would I want to know the secrets to well behaved teenager? See what I mean when I say that NO ONE is getting it, that everything you know about marketing is wrong?

If you have a teenager that embarrasses you in public, that is basically uncontrollable and unmanageable, then aren't you desperate for a solution for that behavior?

So what if the child psychologist used this headline:

Are You Sick And Tired Of The Yelling, Screaming & Belligerent Attitude Of Your Teenager?

Doesn't that immediately address the conversation going on in the heads of these parents. Won't that headline immediately interrupt them and knock them out of downtime and into uptime? Of course it will.

Consider this example of a moving company who were a client of one of my own business coaches in America. Now, yes this is an American example but remember the marketing equation works no matter where you are, or what language you speak because like you've discovered it's based on human nature. Most movers' ads and websites have headlines that say something brilliant like, "Moving."

Most of them have their company name for the headline along the top of their website and marketing material or "local and long-distance."

Why in the world would you ever say something like that? However, by changing their marketing so it followed the marketing equation their new ad and web copy pulled an astounding 12 times more than their original ad.

They went from averaging just 70 calls per month to 955 calls? And their conversion rate skyrocketed from 16% to 68%. Let me put this another way.

This moving company just by changing what their ad said went from generating 11 sales per month to a whopping 649 sales per month.

Their new ad generated so much new business they had to partner with four of their competitors to help them handle the demand for their services.

Oh by the way, those same four competitors bought out that moving company nine months later for €2 million Euros. All due to following the marketing equation in their marketing. So what exactly was it that generated these fantastic results?

Well, their new ad and website featured a headline that said this: "Last year, over 4,350 complaints and lawsuits were filed against moving companies."

Got your attention? You bet, because it hits on the prospect's hot buttons of uncertainty and problems that might arise when they move. Then they go on to describe what to look for and what to watch out for when moving.

It educates the prospect as to what standards they should use to find the best value when hiring a moving company. Ok, to wrap up this discussion about interrupt and engage, let me address the topic of engage specifically for just a moment.

To successfully engage, all you have to do is use a headline or a sub-headline that promises the reader that, if they will keep reading or listening to the ad, that they will get information that will facilitate their making the best decision possible.

Not sales information... not "here's how great we are" information but rather bona fide decision-facilitating information. Sometimes the headline itself will engage, but more frequently it's a sub-headline that makes the promise to educate and therefore engages.

Let's go back to the childcare ad and continue that example. Remember the one that had the headline that said:

Ever Felt Like Your Childcare Treated Your Child Like A Number Instead Of A Little Person?

The follow-up engage sub-headline would simply say:

How To Ensure Your Child Gets Personal, Loving, Caring, One-On-One Attention At Childcare.

Or the headline that said:

Is Your Childcare's Idea Of Good Educational Curriculum Watching Doc McStuffins on TV?

The follow-up headline that engages says:

How Would You Like Your Child To Be Reading at First Class Level Before Starting School?

 In both cases, these sub-headlines clarify the first headline and let the reader know that, if they keep reading the ad, they can expect to find specific details regarding each of these major hot button issues. In short, these sub-headlines engage.

The child psychologist that used the headline:

Are You Sick And Tired Of The Yelling, Screaming & Belligerent Attitude Of Your Teenager?

His sub-headline said this:

Now You Can Discover The Secrets To Controlling Your Teenager And Instantly Restore Peace And Quiet In Your Home.

Show me just ONE parent experiencing this sort of behavior from their own child who wouldn't immediately respond to this ad.

 The moving ad -- remember they had the headline, "Last year, over 4,350 complaints and lawsuits were filed against moving companies"? -- It had a sub-headline that reads as follows:

"Ask these 15 questions to make sure that your moving company's policies, procedures, and standards will protect you from an unpleasant moving experience."

So what do you think you might find if you decide to keep reading the rest of this ad or website? That's right: 15 things to be aware of and to look for when choosing a mover. The sub-headline engages the reader to continue reading to find out the decision-facilitating information.

And that brings us to the third and fourth components of the marketing equation: educate and offer. Like we discussed in depth, every marketing piece should contain a risk-lowering offer to encourage the prospect to take the next step and that offer should generally be to receive additional information, or in other words, to further educate the prospect, and to build your case.

The Truth!

The Real Key to Success in Marketing

"See things in the present, even if they are in the future."

- Larry Ellison

Now here's the real key to success in marketing. The right offer allows you to capture a large percentage of all future buyers in addition to those looking to buy right now.

There's an educational process that the prospect goes through from the moment they begin thinking about buying your product or service... to the point where they actually complete the purchase.

Most marketing only caters to those now-buyers who'll be making a purchase decision in the very near future... and does nothing or very little to educate those who are just thinking about it right now but who might buy later. Here's the problem with that.

At any given moment, the number of prospects who are ready to buy right now represent no more than 1-5% of all those who are ultimately going to buy what you sell.

You've got 95-99% of your prospects who are in the thinking-about-it and gathering-information mode, but when they're attempting to gather information, you don't give it to them!

This is where the fourth component of the marketing equation becomes absolutely huge. Your offer gives you the opportunity to provide additional, educational information to the gathering-information-mode prospects and, in the process, capture valuable information about who these people are so that you can proactively market to them on an ongoing basis. This allows you to take total control of your target market.

The childcare that we've been talking about makes a perfect example of this. How many of the parents that see that ad for childcare remember the one that says, Ever Felt Like Your Childcare Treated Your Child Like A Number Instead Of A Little Person? Or the one that said: Is Your Childcare's Idea Of Good Educational Curriculum Watching Doc McStuffins on TV? Remember those?

How many of those readers do you think are ready and waiting to relocate their kid from their current childcare to this childcare and were relieved to see this ad so they could finally make the switch?

My guess: maybe 1% maximum are now-buyers. But because the headline, sub-headline, and images are so powerful... because they do such a good job of interrupting and engaging... a lot more parents who are not ready to buy right this minute are going to see those ads, pay attention, and be interested.

These powerful ads could easily compel as many as 10... 15... or even 25% of the parents who read these ads to seriously contemplate changing childcare services.

But if the ad's only offer is the typical one that most childcares put in their ads -- "call for a free consultation" -- then none of those future buyers are going to call.

Why would they?

If you're not ready to make a change, why on Earth would you call now for a free consultation? You wouldn't! Furthermore, the ad itself is relatively limited in size.

The childcare can't possibly cram their entire case with all of its associated evidence right there in the ad. It won't fit!

This is why we would recommend that the childcare provide

what we call an informational offer.

What if they offered everyone who calls a free report titled 10 Things Your Childcare May Not Tell You! This report uncovers the 10 critical areas all parents <u>must</u> know and investigate before they place their kids with anyone offering childcare services.

This revealing report compares the 17 most popular area childcares against each other in all 10 of these areas saving the parents their time, effort and energy when making that all important decision as to who will watch their child.

But here's the really neat part by having this type of offer. When the parents do call in, or go online to request the free report, the childcare can now capture that prospect's contact information and proactively market to them from now until forever.

Then the childcare could set up what we call a drip campaign to consistently and repetitiously follow up with these interested parents and keep providing them with additional decision-making information until they finally become ready to buy.

Depending on what you sell and the specific situation, there are actually eight different types of informational offers that we create and offer your prospects. And if we want to dominate your marketplace, we've got to get your offers right as well. Hopefully, this is all coming together for you now.

How to start implementing this in your business tomorrow

"Risk more than others think is safe. Dream more than others think is practical."

-    Howard Schultz

In this next section of The Truth I want to give you some actionable 'how to' information based on everything we discussed and implement it into your business. Now that you have the background on the fundamentals, we're going to focus on implementing those fundamentals into your business now, step by step.

In this section of the book we will cover:

- How to define your target market, if you haven't already
- How to strengthen your marketing message
- How to generate more leads with less effort
- How to create marketing materials that are profitable
- How to craft powerful offers
- How to write headlines that stop your prospects in their tracks
- How to write ads that sell

This section is just a mere snippet of the wealth of knowledge and systems I have waiting for you inside the Truth members area (www.wrong.ie) and in my other training programs and memberships. If you find value in these, don't delay in reaching out to get access. Any investment needed is dwarfed by the extraordinary value provided.

How to Identify Your Target Market

"It's hard to target a message to a generic 35-year-old middle-class working mother of two. It's much easier to target a message to Jennifer, who has two children under four, works as a paralegal, and is always looking for quick but healthy dinners and ways to spend more time with her kids and less time on housework."

- Elizabeth Gardener

Qualified leads are the group of people who are most likely to buy from you - they have a current need, problem or desire that your offering will solve or serve. These people are your target market, or ideal customers. Qualified leads are generally easier to convert into customers, so a high number of qualified leads mean a high conversion rate and, of course, more sales.

A great example of this going wrong... you own a burger business and are standing outside a large convention, waiting for the lunch-break to take advantage of a huge rush of people in a short period of time (a great way to do business) to give away small hotdogs to generate customers for your business down the road.

You have prepared all your toppings, flyers with simple directions, arranged for staff to handle the rush and stocked up mightily to ensure you do not miss a single prospect. The group comes out and you manage 25 free hot dogs given away when you were expecting 500.

What went wrong? You did not realize the convention was a health and wellness group comprising of 95% vegetarians... morale of the story; if you are talking to the wrong audience it doesn't matter how good your offer is - you are wasting your time. Talking to your target market is absolutely CRITICAL to successful marketing.

So, your first job as a business owner now that you understand the marketing equation is to figure out who your target market is, and how the people in it think and behave.

In this chapter we will cover:

- How your target market influences your marketing choices
- A step-by-step process for identifying your target market
- Types of target markets
- Examples of target markets
- Market research strategies

Generating qualified leads will make it easy to boost your conversion rate, because your prospects will already want or need your service.

A target market is simply a group of people with something in common - things like age, gender, opinion, interest, or location, - who will purchase a particular product or service. Your market can be broad or specific in scope, and it is unique to each business or industry.

Knowledge and understanding of your target market is crucial to the viability of your business. You have to know if there is enough demand for your product, or enough interest and need for your service. You have to know how to communicate with your customers, and understand their thoughts and behaviors.

Without a comprehensive understanding of your target market, you can't make smart choices about your front end offers, marketing strategy, pricing structure, and product or service mix. It's kind of like driving a car with a blindfold on - you'd be headed for disaster.

In addition to being essential to confirm assumptions and understand purchase motivations, market research is something you will need to get into the habit of doing on a regular basis to monitor trends and stay ahead of the competition. Identifying your target market is not always easy, but I promise it will pay off in spades, so stay committed to your efforts as you work through this chapter.

Let's start with an easy, step-by-step process to identify your target market. You likely already have an idea of who your target market is - or who you want it to be. Start by describing who you think your target market is in two or three sentences on your pad of paper.

As you work through this process, you may find that you were correct in your assumptions, or not. Either way, this chapter will discover invaluable information about your audience.

When you set out to identify your target market, you need to find the group of people that has these four characteristics:

- They have a particular need, want or desire.
- They have the financial ability to purchase your solution to their need, want or desire.
- They have the power to decide to purchase your product or service.
- They have access to your business, through a physical location, Internet or catalogue

First, take a look at what it is you offer or provide your customers. To find the group of people with the characteristics listed above, you first need to answer the following questions about your product or service:

1. What is the need, want or desire that my product or services fulfill?

Does your offering primarily fulfill a desire, or serve a need or cater to a want? What is it?

2. What does my product or service cost?

Do you offer a high-end product, or low-cost alternative? Do you sell large items, like a kitchen appliance, or small items, like household cleaning products?

3. Who makes the decision to purchase my product or service (who has the power or authority)?

For example, if you provide a product or service for children, their parents are the people who make the decision to make a purchase

4. How are my products or services accessed?

Does your ideal customer need to live in the same city or region as your business? Or can they access your products online, or through a catalogue?

Now let's look at the demographic and psychographic characteristics of the people that need, can afford access and decide to purchase your offering.

Demographics:

Answer the following demographic questions about the people who use your product. Some of the demographic information in this table may be less important than the rest (like ethnicity or religion) depending on your product or service and the market you're trying to attract.

The Truth!

Age: *In general terms, what is the age range that my product or service caters to? Kids? Teens? Adults? Seniors?*

Income: *How much do they have to make to afford my product? Is this single or double household income? Low? Medium? High?*

Gender: *Does my product or service appeal to men, women, or both?*

Generation: *What is the generation of my customers? Based on the age range I identified, are they baby boomers? GenX? GenY? Where do they stand in the overall family life cycle?*

Nationality: *Is nationality relevant to my product or service?*

Ethnicity: *Is ethnicity relevant to my product or service?*

Marital Status: *Are my customers married? Single? Divorced?*

Family Size: *Does my product or service cater to large or small families? Is family size relevant?*

Occupation or Industry: *Does my product or service appeal to people in a certain occupation, or industry?*

Religion: *Is religion relevant to my product or service?*

Language: *Is language relevant to my product or service?*

Education: *What level of education do my primary customers have? Secondary? University?*

Psychographics

Answer the following questions on your target market's psychographics. Psychographics are the qualitative characteristics of your target audience, like personality, values, attitudes, interests, or lifestyle. These characteristics can give you a lot of insight into how to best interact and communicate with your target market.

Lifestyle: *What kind of lifestyle group does your audience fall into? Are they conservative or trendy, travelers or soccer moms? Are they thrifty or extravagant?*

Values + Beliefs: *What are their values and beliefs? Would you consider them environmentalists or safety conscious?*

Attitude: *What kind of attitude do they have? Are they positive or negative? Open or critical? Easily led or opinionated?*

Motivation: *Are your customers opinion leaders or followers? Do they tell others what products they need, or do they need others to tell them what is trendy and what works?*

Activities + Interests: *What do they do in their spare time? What are their hobbies and interests?*

Social Class: *What social class does your audience belong to? Lower, middle or upper? How much extra money do they have to spend on luxury items?*

The Truth!

So, now that you've gathered all this information, what does it tell you about your ideal customers?

You've done enough research now to create a picture of who you think your ideal customer is. Being as specific as you can, write a 1-2 sentence statement about your target market.

For example:

My target customer is a successful young professional; a middle-class man aged 20 to 35, who is single, makes more than €50,000 per year, and is physically fit. He is university educated, and has an active interest in economics and politics.

My target market is affluent new mothers; married women with children under five years old, between the ages of 25 and 45, and have a household income of at least €100,000 annually. She is the trend and opinion follower, and her purchase motivations are driven by her peer group.

Now that you've made some educated assumptions about who your target market is, you'll have to use some market research strategies to confirm them.

Market research is the study of a particular group of consumers - or markets. It is one of the most valuable activities you will work on as a business owner, since it keeps you connected and informed about your customers thoughts, motivations and behaviors. Market research also minimizes risk and assumption-based decision making, which will improve the success rate of everything you do for your business.

When you begin your market research, you need to start out with a clear question that you want answered. Otherwise, you'll quickly get off track and fail to end up with the information you really need. Think about questions like:

- Am I right about my target audience assumptions?
- Is my target audience interested in my new product or service?
- I need more information about my target audience's purchase motivations
- What new trends are my target audience following?
- What recent economic developments have impacted my target market?
- How can I improve my customer service?
- Has my target market changed in the past year?

Market research needs to be conducted regularly - regardless of how long you have been in business, or how well you know your target market. Trends shift, and environments are impacted by economic and political factors beyond your control.

There are two main types of market research - primary and secondary - and three main areas of market research - consumer, competitor, and environment.

Here's a really helpful chart to use to organize information when you're conducting your market research. This will help you conduct research that is comprehensive and cost effective.

	CUSTOMER (The demographic, behavioristic, psychographic and geographic characteristics of your customers.)	COMPETITION (The marketing, product and consumer observations you can make or gather from your competition.)	ENVIRONMENT (The social, economic and political trends that may impact your business or your customers thoughts and behaviors.)
SECONDARY (Second-hand data or research that has been completed by and for someone else, but can be applied to your objectives.)	> statistics > trade journals > public surveys by larger companies > government publications and surveys		> newspapers > trade journals > consumer reports
PRIMARY (First-hand information gathered from your customers or about your customers. i.e., customer surveys, observations about the competition, etc.)	> info right from the source > can be time consuming and costly - but most valuable > most current > most specific	> what works, what doesn't > adding value to existing offering - thus giving yourself an edge > types of products that consumers are interested in > note the types of lead generation strategies your competition uses, and the types of potential customers that you see in the store	

Strategies for cost-effective secondary market research:

Demographic Research (Customer)
Basic demographic research is something you won't have to conduct yourself. Every city, town or region will have demographic information available online, or in city halls, libraries and business centers. National and regional statistical information is also available online or at government agencies.

Online and Consumer Research (Customer and Environment)
Primary market research can be expensive, so secondary research on general consumer behavior and purchase data can be extremely useful for small businesses. Some information will be available online, while other information (usually free)

will be available at your local chamber of commerce and business centres.

Primary market research strategies you shouldn't miss:

Ground Research (Customer or Competition)
Spend some time in your local area at different times of the day observing and talking to the people who live, work, or spend time there. What do you notice about the neighbourhood? How well is it taken care of? Why do people spend time here? Is anything missing? Get a sense of their age, gender, clothing and any other features.

Competing Businesses (Competition)
If you have direct competitors in the same local area, spend some time being "their" customer and making observations about their business. How do they advertise? What market are they targeting? Is there a niche market that is being missed?

Surveys (Customer or Competition)
Surveys are the most popular way to gather first hand information from your existing and potential customers. Take your time to administer them carefully and thoughtfully - surveys can get complex and variables can be high.

Keep your questionnaire short and focused on soliciting the information you need to answer your market research question. This will encourage a higher response rate. Remember that your information will only be as good as the people you ask for it. Try to get as broad a cross section as possible. Depending on your market research question, you may not want to limit it to your existing customers.
Choose a survey method - telephone, web or paper-based - and understand the pros and cons of each. Research some survey templates, and spend more time than you think you need to on crafting your survey.

Include basic demographic questions on your survey so you can cross reference responses with factors like age, income, sex, and profession.

Website Analysis (Customer)
Use a website tracking system like Google Analytics to monitor how visitors to your website behave and use the information available. These programs will allow you to see how many people visit your site, where they are from, what pages they are looking at and how long they spend on your site.

Customer Loyalty and Purchase Data (Customer)
Your point of sale system - depending on the level of features it offers - may also be able to run reports on customer purchase patterns and trends. If you have a customer loyalty program, you can keep track of purchase information in each customer's file or account. The type of information you'll need to keep track of here is behavioristic: brand loyalty, product usage, purchase frequency, and readiness to buy.

Focus Groups (Customer)
Assemble groups of six to 12 people and ask them general and specific questions about their thoughts, opinions and habits as related to your marketing question. Be sure to assemble a cross section of people that is representative of your target market.

When you've completed your market research, analyze what you've learned. Go back to your original question, and weigh the outcome.

How has your market research supported the question(s) you set out to answer? Were your original assumptions confirmed or refuted?

- Does my target market exist in my geographic area?
- Does my target market actually want what I'm selling?
- How does my target market want to purchase from me?

- Is my target market interested in my new product or service?
- How does my target market want me to communicate with them?
- Is my target market large enough in my local area to support my business?
- Are there areas of my research I could dig into for more information?

You may discover some hard facts to face about your business. Perhaps there is not a large enough market base in your area to support your business. Maybe you've spent thousands of dollars going after the wrong type of customers. This is all okay - it's valuable information that you can work with to make better decisions about your marketing strategies and product or service offerings.

If you have flexibility in your product or service, you may be able to find ways to enhance your offerings and extend your target market to include more people, or a larger share of the marketplace.

Your market research is ongoing - each time you talk to a customer, supplier or sales rep, you're gathering information about your clientele, and thus conducting market research.

Remember, audiences, trends, products and services change, so stay ahead of the curve and keep on top of your market.

Plan to make market research a regular part of your business, and schedule time and money for primary research at least once a year. This is the only way to stay ahead of the competition when it comes to trends and environmental changes beyond your control.

The next few chapters are about applying the information you have learned about your target market to refine your marketing strategies. You've clearly identified who your target market is, and how those people think and behave, so your next task is to determine what to say and how to reach them.

In the next chapter, we're going to look at your marketing message and how clearly you're communicating with your audience. As we discussed, the strength of your marketing message is the backbone of your marketing materials, and a huge factor in the success of lead generation strategies.

Strengthening your marketing message

"Think like a customer."

- Paul Gillin

The strength of your marketing message lies in its ability to speak to the specific wants and desires of your target market, and tap into their emotional reactions, or hot buttons.

When you push those hot buttons, you motivate your audience to take action. The more people you can motivate to take action, the more leads you'll have in store and on the other end of the phone line.

In this chapter we will cover:

- How a strong marketing message will supercharge your lead generation
- Examples of strong marketing messages
- A step-by-step process for developing your unique marketing message
- Strategies that will strengthen your existing marketing message
- How to test and measure the strength of your message.
- How to be consistent with your strong marketing message
- A strong marketing message will make a huge difference in your lead generation strategies.

A marketing message is simply a statement or phrase that you use to communicate information about your business to others.

A strong marketing message will do four things:
- Speak to the reader's needs, wants or problems (hot buttons)

The Truth!

- Offer a solution, advantage or benefit
- Describe a point of difference
- Motivate the reader to take action

As I said earlier, the key here is to motivate your target audience to do something after they read or hear the message. It needs to be strong enough to entice the audience to ask for more information, visit the website, pick up the phone or walk in the store.

You will put your marketing message on every piece of marketing material your business uses for lead generation, so it has to be powerful and consistent and speak to the group of people that you have identified as your ideal customers. Strengthening your marketing message has the potential to dramatically increase your lead generation before you even change your existing strategies.

Here are some examples of strong marketing messages that are used by successful businesses today. The most famous one and one that I use again and again is Dominos pizza.

Domino's Pizza: You get fresh, hot pizza delivered to your door in 30 minutes or less -- or it's free!

M&Ms: The milk chocolate melts in your mouth, not in your hand.

Enterprise Rent-A-Car: We'll pick you up.

FedEx: When it absolutely, positively has to be there overnight.

Jeweler: Don't pay 300% markups to a traditional jeweler for inferior diamonds! We guarantee that your loose diamond will appraise for at least 200% of the purchase price, or we'll buy it back.

Dentist   : We guarantee that you will have a comfortable experience and never have to wait more than 15 minutes or you will receive a free exam.

Real Estate: Our 20 Step Marketing System Will Sell Your House In Less Than 45 Days At Full Market Value.

Let's get started with the process you can use to create a new marketing message for your business, or refine the marketing message you already have.

Work through the following questions to brainstorm and record the aspects of your business that you will communicate in your marketing message. Take your time, and be as detailed as possible.

1. Use all the information you can on your target market to figure out what your customer's hot buttons are.

Write down who your customers are, and what their problems, desires and needs are.

Take some time to revisit the behavioral and psychographic information you gathered when researching your target market. This will give you an idea of what kind of emotional hot buttons you should focus on when creating your marketing message.

Hot buttons are emotional triggers that motivate your potential customers to take action. Some common hot buttons are: price, location, exclusivity, results, safety, timeliness, convenience and atmosphere.

2. Describe the value or benefit that your product or service offers your customers.

This is what your customers get when they spend money at your business - the answer to "what's in it for me?" How do you solve their problems? How do you meet their needs, or fulfill their desires?

For example, maybe you're a grocery store in the neighbourhood, and you offer the convenience of being just a short stroll away instead of a car ride.

When you're thinking about this question, think about your product or service in the context of the benefits, results, or advantages customers receive, instead of the features you offer.

3. Think about the outcome of the value or solution that you provide.

Brainstorm what happens when your customers receive the value or benefit from your product or service, what happens? Are they thrilled? Relieved of worry? Do they have more time to spend with their families, or do they put dinner on the table faster?

This is kind of like the storytelling aspect of creating your marketing message. Paint a picture of how you will improve the lives of your customers, in one way or another.

4. What is your company's point of difference? What makes you stand out from the competition?

Your point of difference - or uniqueness - is something you will want to strongly feature in your marketing message. It is the reason that the reader should choose your business instead of your competition.

For this step, do some research on your competition and see what kinds of marketing messages they are using. How strong are those messages? What benefits and results do they promise?

If you are having trouble figuring out what sets you apart from your competition, think about including an irresistible offer, or a strong guarantee to give yourself an edge. (We'll spend some time on powerful offers and risk reversal strategies like guarantees later on in the program.)

5. What is the perception you would like others to have about your business?

How you wish your customers to perceive you will impact how you describe your offering in your marketing message, and the kind of language you will use. Revisit the vision you created, and write down some ideas about the image you want your business to project to the outside world.

For example, if your business is completely transforming its operations to become more environmentally sustainable, you will need to use different language and emphasize different features and benefits than you did before.

6. Based on the notes you wrote in response to the above questions, summarize the information into a paragraph of 4 to 5 sentences.

If you've got pages of notes, this may be a challenging part of the process, but that's okay because it means you have a lot to work with. Take your time, and wade through your notes bit by bit.

You may want to start by writing 10 to 15 sentences, and then narrow those down to 4 to 5 sentences when you have a better idea of what specifically you want to focus on. Or, you could try writing three sentences for each question, and then working to synthesize from that point.

Keep in mind that the most effective marketing messages use strong, descriptive language that triggers emotional responses. Think about how you would describe your point of difference, or value-added service to a close friend, and write with that in mind.

7. Using descriptive language, synthesize your paragraph into a single sentence of 15 words or less.

This sentence will become your unique marketing message!

I know how challenging this part of the process can be, so to make it easier, I usually write a few different sentences that emphasize different things to give myself choices. For example, if you don't know whether to feature your company's commitment to unbelievable prices, or its guarantee of customer satisfaction, write one sentence each and compare which is stronger.

Aim to have two or three sentences that you're happy with, and then test them out to see which is the most effective.

The only way to find out the strength of your marketing message is to test it. Don't be afraid of making some mistakes - you need to get feedback!

Test your three draft marketing messages internally first.

Before you go out to the public with your drafts, test them on your friends, family, staff and colleagues first. Use their feedback constructively, but don't be afraid to stand up for elements that you believe are effective or important.

Once you have gathered enough feedback, rework your draft messages and incorporate the suggestions you believe are valuable.

Incorporate feedback, and then test a few draft messages externally.

When you have refined your draft messages and incorporated staff and colleague feedback, you can start to test the messages out on your audience.

This doesn't have to be complicated, or cost a lot of money. Simple tests using small-scale distributions will give you the information you need to choose which message is the most effective.

For example, place two or three ads in the local newspaper - one a week with a different message each time - and compare the number of leads each ad generates. Or, send out a small direct mail campaign, with the materials split into three groups - one for each message. If online, you could drive some paid traffic to a landing page that conveys your message.

The message that generates the most leads is the strongest, and will be the one you choose to be your business' unique marketing message.

Now that you've got a killer message, use it consistently on all of your marketing materials and in all of your campaigns.

Consistency and repetition are powerful persuasive tools to use to reinforce your message over time. Ensuring your marketing message appears on all documents related to your business will build your brand image and your company's reputation.

Make a list of all marketing materials, stationery, signage and internal and external documentation that your customers and clients come in contact with. Then, incorporate your marketing message onto each of them.

Here's a suggested list of materials to include:

- Website
- Advertisements
- Direct Mail

- Listings
- Voicemail messages
- Email Signature
- Business Cards
- Letterhead

Now that you know what you're going to say, and who you're going to say it to, let's dive into some lead generation strategies.

The next chapter focuses on advanced strategies for lead generation that you can start implementing into your business right away. Our focus is to set up lead generation strategies that either immediately or over time will run themselves, so you can generate more leads with less time investment.

How to Generate More Leads With Less Effort

"The aim of marketing is to know and understand the customer so well the product or service fits him and sells itself."

- Peter Drucker

What is the current picture of lead generation and management in your business?

Here's the deal: in order to start generating more leads with less time and financial investment, you first have to spend time setting up systems and making some changes.

Your goal in this chapter is to establish a solid lead tracking and lead management system, and make small tweaks to your existing lead generation strategies based on the work you completed in the target market and marketing message chapters.

They're many different lead generation strategies that you can use but I want you to see the impact that the work you have already done will have on your existing strategies. I want you to start seeing results tomorrow.

In this chapter we will cover:

- The current status of lead generation in your company
- The purpose of lead tracking and management systems
- Types of lead tracking and lead management systems
- How to set up a lead tracking and or management system
- Qualified lead generation
- How to get more results from your existing strategies

The Truth!

Do you know where your current leads are coming from, or how many you get on a daily, weekly, or by-campaign basis?

If I asked you to tell me right now what your top lead generation strategies are, what would you say?

A big part of step-one is gaining a solid understanding of where your business stands right now in terms of lead generation. Otherwise, how are you going to know when your lead generation strategies are working? Or which strategies are working?

In a few minutes, I'm going to show you how to set up a lead tracking and lead management system that works with your business. But first, I'd like you to write down (on your pad of paper) what you think your top three lead generation strategies are right now.

Every business needs a lead tracking and management system. Do you have one in place?

A lead tracking and management system is absolutely essential to your business for a number of reasons.

One, it is the only way to know which marketing strategies are working, and which ones aren't. The information your system gathers will allow you to make educated decisions about marketing campaigns and investments.

Two, it organizes your sales and marketing efforts and manages contact information in a user-friendly way. It's clear who you called, when, what you said, and when you said you'd follow up.

Three, it enables you to manage your sales staff by tracking their progress on several leads at once. You'll have access to an at-a-glance picture of their sales figures and productivity.

Your lead tracking system needs to:

- record the leads that arrive by phone, in-store visit, and website visit
- track the source of each lead over specific time periods
- record pertinent customer information
- be simple enough to be used by all staff members

Your lead management system needs to:

- track your leads through the sales plan or process
- increase customer communications or contact
- keep track of correspondences and follow-up requirements
- make it easier for you and your staff to close more sales

Here is a list of information you will want to gather from your leads.

Depending on the needs of your business and the lead tracking and management system you choose (i.e., do you need a mailing address, or just email address?) some of these items may be optional fields. However, I highly recommend you capture full contact details so you can implement the holy grail of marketing – multi step multi-media marketing campaigns using both online and offline.

- Company Name
- Name of Contact
- Alternate Contact Person
- Mailing Address
- Phone Number
- Fax Number
- Cell Phone
- Email Address
- Website Address
- Product of Interest
- Source of Lead (i.e., How did you hear from us?)

- Reason for Enquiry

If it is appropriate for your business, you also may wish to gather demographic information from your leads - but keep this voluntary. This information would be ideally used in your market research analysis.

Keep in mind that your lead tracking and management systems need to be simple enough for everyone in your company to use.

Unless you are the only person in your company who manages incoming phone calls, greets customers and chases down leads, the systems you implement will need to be used consistently by everyone in your organization.

Once you have decided on a system, schedule enough time to train your staff thoroughly and be open to feedback. Since you're not the sole user, you'll need to consider their thoughts on the usability of the systems.

Pick a lead tracking and management system that suits your budget, and offers the features your business needs.

Each business will have different requirements when it comes to lead tracking and management. A retail store will have different needs than a realtor's office, for example.

The retail store may only need to record leads based on lead generation strategies, and keep lead information for their direct mail or newsletter databases. On the other hand, the realtor will need to make contact with their leads on several occasions, and need a system that will record and remind them of those correspondences.

Software for lead management ranges from simple to highly sophisticated, and can be a great investment depending on the needs of your business. Some CRM (Customer Relationship

Management) tools are available online as a web-based system you can subscribe to and have access to on the road.

I've listed the features and advantages to a number of different systems below - ranging from low-tech to high-tech, paper-based to web-savvy.

Index Cards
- Variety of sizes: 3x5, 4X6 or 5X8
- Basic contact information on one side
- Notes on the other side
- Easy to organize and sort

This is a basic system used to manage leads by those who may be less comfortable with computers. This system will be effective at tracking low volumes of leads.

Rolodex
- More contacts than index card system
- Easily organized and compact
- Basic contact information on one side
- Notes on the other side

Another basic system that will effectively manage leads without the use of a computer. While this system can store a higher number of cards, it is also only effective for tracking low volumes of leads.

Excel Spreadsheets
- Electronic system that is highly customizable by date, name, source or other variables
- Easily organized and analyzed
- Several worksheets in a single file allow leads to be tracked and contact managed
- Accessible for those with basic computer skills

This is a slightly more sophisticated system that will allow you to track higher volumes of leads, and effectively organize the information that you collect into charts that can be analyzed.

In Excel, you are able to work with a number of tracking sheets in a single file, and create hard copy tracking sheets for staff to use at point of sale and reception.

Excel also has the capability of importing data from Outlook.

Database Management Programs:
- High level of organization
- Unlimited space for notes and record-keeping
- Data-entry required
- Examples include: MS Outlook, MS Excel

This would be a more sophisticated system that will interface with Excel and manage high volumes of leads and customer details.

Manages distribution lists for newsletters and direct mail campaigns.

Primarily manages contact information, and provides space for notes, follow-ups and reminders.

Tracking high volumes of leads without recording and inputting customer information is best done in Excel.

Customer Relationship Management (CRM) Software:

- Web-based, and accessible from anywhere with internet access
- Organizes leads and customers by name, company, date, or status
- Ability to attach documents (like proposals and contracts) to leads
- Ability to write notes and log correspondence by date

- View contact history and status
- Ability to execute in depth marketing campaigns
- Example is Infusionsoft

When it comes to a CRM that can do it all I cannot recommend infusionsoft enough. It's like having an army of minions constantly working hard for you and your business. Infusionsoft was designed to enable you to implement direct response marketing campaigns into your business with ease. For more on infusionsoft visit www.JohnMulry.com/infusion

Tracks a high volume of relationship-based leads, and provides a detailed, feature-heavy system for lead management.

Not ideal for retail businesses, or businesses that need to track a high volume of leads with minimal customer information attached.

Website Analytics:
- Monitors and analyzes website traffic and online advertising
- Tracks number of people who visit your site, where they came from (search engines, online advertisement, website link etc.), how long they stayed, the pages they visited, and which page they left the site from.
- Google Analytics is an easy-to-use example

An ideal way to track and analyze website traffic to complement your overall lead tracking system. This is not a complete system on its own.

This requires the insertion of a specific code into each of your web-pages, or each of your online advertisements. It allows you to monitor usage statistics, and generates reports, charts, graphs, etc.

Bringing qualified leads into your business will save you and your sales team time, and result in higher revenues.

Qualified leads are simply the potential customers who are the most likely to buy your product or service. They're not just in your store taking at look at the latest features in refrigerators; they're in the market to purchase a refrigerator. They're not wandering in to see what a €500 handbag looks like; they are the kind of person who can actually spend €500 on a handbag.

Some of the people who will call you or visit your business will never buy from you no matter how good your sales scripts are or how much time you spend overcoming their objectives. There are a variety of reasons for this - and you'll never eliminate all of these people - but you will need to focus on bringing in more of the people who are ready to buy.

The good news is you have spent so much time and energy cultivating a comprehensive knowledge of your target market, that you're in a great position to increase the number of qualified leads you bring into your business.

How do You Get Qualified Leads?

The crux of qualified lead generation is making decisions based on the market research you completed on your target market. You basically need to know where to reach your market, and how to speak to them.

When you are designing, executing and making choices about your lead generation strategies, always consider these questions.

Who is my target market? Write down your target market description to keep you focused on the specifics of this group of people.

DISTRIBUTION IS EVERYTHING: How does my target market like to receive information? Do they read the newspaper? Pick up the family mail? Spend hours on

Facebook? Subscribe to any magazines/publications? Listen to news radio on long commutes to work?

What motivates my target market to take action, and how can I tap into that motivation? How will you tap into your target market's emotional response? What issues or needs will mean something to them, and drive them into your store to solve them.

Where can I place my marketing message so my target market will see it? Look at what you found out in your market research about your target market's hobbies, activities and interests. How can you place your message or your product or service in their path?

What can I offer my target market to entice them to purchase from me? Can you offer your target market something special, rare, or time specific that will appeal only to them?

I'm going to show you how some little changes will generate big results for your company in short order.

Once you're set up with a testing and measuring system (your lead tracking and management systems) to evaluate the success of your lead generation strategies, you need to start by looking for opportunities to juice up the strategies you're currently working with.

1. **Use your new marketing message:** Make sure that you have put your new marketing message on all of your marketing materials, where new and existing customers can see it. Revise your standard advertisements to feature the strengthened copy.
2. **Strengthen your offer:** Create an offer that's too good to refuse - not for your entire target market, but for your ideal customer. How can you cater to their unique needs and wants? What will be irresistible for them?

3. **Refocus your direct mail campaign.** If you're sending your direct mail to entire locations and areas, stop and refocus. If your distribution area is that broad, chances are the copy on your postcard or letter is too broad as well. Brainstorm ways to narrow your distribution and only hit your target audience. Purchase consumer lists based on demographics, not just location, or limit distribution to specific housing types. Of course, make sure you rework the direct mail piece to feature your marketing message.

4. **Let your target market's behaviors dictate your distribution plans.** As I discussed above, the more you can tailor your strategy to the needs and habits of your target market, the strong your results will be. Look for opportunities in your existing direct mail, advertising, flyer drop and other strategies to get specific. Narrow the demographics of your list, or place an ad in a niche publication. Brainstorm new ways to target your market's emotional reactions.

5. **Tap into low-cost advertising.** Advertising in places like the Facebook, Google Adwords, classifieds sections, e-mail newsletters and even the forgotten Bing can be a great place to test your marketing message for minimal investment.

6. **Look for some referral business.** Referral business is desirable because it usually brings qualified leads into your business. Someone has referred them to you based on a current need or desire.
    - ➢ Provide your customers with an incentive to bring business to you. Reward successful referrals with discounts or gifts.
    - ➢ Create a referral chain by giving each new customer three free coupons for products or services that they can give to their friends. When their friends come into your business, do the same.
    - ➢ Create complementary alliances with non-competitor businesses with the same target market. Cross-

promotion or cross-referral strategies will benefit both businesses.

7. Website sign-up Add a feature on your website that encourages visitors to sign-up for newsletters or other communications. You can also set up your website so that potential customers need to fill out a simple form before they have access to "free" information.

Stop using strategies that don't work.

Now that you have a comprehensive lead tracking system in place, you'll be able to track the leads that each strategy is responsible for generating.

When you complete your first few campaigns with the lead tracking system and analyze the numbers, compare the results to the initial predictions you made. Were you correct in your assumptions, or were you surprised by how things shook out.

The purpose of testing and measuring using a lead tracking system is to figure out which strategies work, and which don't, as well as which strategies work best, and which generate mediocre results. This not only will save you money but is incredibly useful information to have when developing marketing budgets and, of course, trying to drive sales.

READ THIS: A quick cautionary note on conversions.

While the focus of this and recent chapters has been lead generation, remember this formula: #leads x %conversion rate = #customers. Don't lose sight of the relationship between leads and conversions in the overall formula. Your conversion rate is equally as important as the number of leads you're bringing in.

Remember that when more leads start flowing through your door, you'll need to have the resources and systems in place to give a high level of customer service and to convert them into loyal customers. You've put effort into generating these qualified leads, but if you don't have the resources in place to give them the attention required, you'll lose them.

Once established, your lead tracking and lead management system should require minimal time investment...if you keep it up to date.

Keep your systems up to date. The biggest pain (and drain on time) is having to go back and enter heaps of data into your database or management system because someone has let it pile up.

It's also a huge missed opportunity! If you fall behind on your lead tracking system, because you won't be able to effectively evaluate your campaign or strategy. Or, you may have missed a lead because you didn't follow-up soon enough.

Creating Marketing Materials That Get Results. Period.

"It's much easier to double your business by doubling your conversion rate than by doubling your traffic."

- Jeff Eisenberg

Your marketing materials are an extension of you and your company. How are yours working?

You can have a lot of fun creating marketing materials for your business. It's an opportunity to work on a project that isn't a spreadsheet, or a graph or an order form. You can really get creative!

Your materials get distributed in the world to send out a particular message (or messages) about your company and what you sell. They're ambassadors for your business because they speak to your potential customers when you're not there.

As you probably know, it's easy to get carried away with marketing collateral. You're surrounded by flashy, clever advertising everywhere you look, and when the time comes to create your own, you can't help but feel that you have to keep up with the joneses.

Most of the time this doesn't work. You spend more money, and see less impressive results. In this chapter, I'm going to show you some proven strategies for simplifying and strengthening your marketing materials, and focusing on the materials you need not the materials you think you think you should have.

In this chapter we will cover:

➢ The marketing materials you really need - and the ones you don't
➢ The mistakes you might be making now
➢ The elements each piece of marketing collateral should have
➢ What you need to know about the design of your materials
➢ What you need to know about testing, measuring and making mistakes
➢ It's easy to want to match your competition piece by piece - but when you're trying to stretch your marketing budget, focus on the materials you actually need.

Just because your competition has an eight page, glossy color brochure, doesn't mean you need one to run a successful business.

When one brochure has the ability to eat your entire budget for marketing materials, you have to prioritize what's essential and what's just a "wish" or want. You need to make sure you're spending on the items that are going to bring in the most return on investment.

Your marketing materials need to communicate your message to your target and motivate them to act. Do you really need a glossy brochure when black and white flyers will be just as effective? Think about this when making decisions about your marketing items.

Make choices based on how your target audience prefers to receive information. Do they prefer paper newsletters, or electronic ones? Are they environmentally conscious, or technology savvy? Do they appreciate personal contact, or just need to see information in a newspaper? Remember that how you communicate is often just as or more important that what you communicate.

What are the marketing materials that your business needs, wants and would like to have?

- ➤ Logo
- ➤ Business Cards
- ➤ Brochure
- ➤ Website
- ➤ Newsletter
- ➤ Catalogue
- ➤ Advertisements
- ➤ Flyers
- ➤ Fridge Magnet
- ➤ Branded Swag (pens, etc.)
- ➤ Employee Clothing
- ➤ Cloth Bags
- ➤ Product Labels
- ➤ Signage
- ➤ Email Signature
- ➤ Blog
- ➤ Letterhead + Envelopes
- ➤ Thank You Cards
- ➤ Notepads
- ➤ Seasonal Gifts
- ➤ Company Profile
- ➤ Internal Templates (Fax Cover, Memo, etc.)

Create a list of your essential marketing materials then, below it, create a list of your "wish" marketing materials. You can use your "wish list" when you have a little extra budget, or are looking to create a "wow" piece. The list above is for you to use as a guideline - you may not need all of these items, or want to add your own ideas to the list.

Take your existing marketing materials through this audit, and look for opportunities to improve and strengthen.

Are you fighting for their attention with a powerful headline?

Like we talked about in depth in the marketing equation section, you have about four seconds to grab the attention of your reader with your headline. If you do, you have a few more seconds to convince them to read your sub-headline. If you're successful in doing that, you have a few more seconds to get them to read further. See what I'm saying?

Make sure your headlines:

> ➢ Offer to take away pain or give pleasure
> ➢ Hit your target market's hot buttons
> ➢ Bring up emotion
> ➢ Are bold, dramatic, shocking or unbelievable
> ➢ Answer the questions - what's in it for the customer? Why should the customer care?

Are you triggering an emotional response to a problem, fear, need or want?

Once you have their attention, you need to continue to keep it. Shake up their confidence in what they're doing now, or the urgency with which they need to solve their problem. Put their fears, concerns and desires in black and white text in front of their eyes:

Ask them if they:

> ➢ Are doing enough?
> ➢ Can wait any longer?
> ➢ Can sacrifice anymore?
> ➢ Are paying too much?
> ➢ Are getting the best product or service for their money?
> ➢ Are you building their trust or confidence in your ability to meet their needs?

You've got their attention, and tapped into their emotions, now you need to build their confidence in you ability to solve their problems and meet their needs. You'll need to show them your solution, and prove that you can be trusted to do what you promise.

Tell them how:

> ➢ You're different from the competition
> ➢ You're highly qualified
> ➢ You have documented results
> ➢ You have a high number of happy customers
> ➢ You get recognized from others in your field
> ➢ Are you wowing them with your competitive edge?

You may be the best at what you do or have the best product but if your customers can't get a hold of you when they need you, how valuable are you? Here are some examples:

Tell them how you do more than the competition:

> ➢ 24-hour customer service
> ➢ House calls, or free delivery
> ➢ Customer rewards program
> ➢ Other convenience services

Are you overcoming their objections before they've raised them?

It makes no difference what business you are in; there will always be objections to buying what you are selling. Most often the biggest objection is the price. You should confront them head-on by explaining why it's worth paying your price. You need to put their fears to rest before they will be ready to buy.

Are you providing an element of risk reversal with a strong guarantee?

Stand behind what you're claiming about the quality of your product or service, and offer a guarantee in your marketing materials. Typically, the strength and length of the guarantee indicate the quality of the product in most customers' eyes, so create a strong one.

You can guarantee:

- ➤ Performance
- ➤ Benefits
- ➤ Longevity
- ➤ Satisfaction

Are you showing them what other people have said about your product or service?

Use testimonials to speak to your credibility and merit. Let the testimonials show your potential clients how trustworthy you are, and how much benefit they've received from your product or service. Make sure the testimonial addresses the problem that your customer had before they used your product.

Are you giving them an easy way to contact you?

Make it easy for customers to be in touch with you, or get more information. Clearly display your phone number and website address on everything you produce, and consider including a map of your store location so you're easy to find.

Are you giving them a reason to act NOW?

The last job your marketing piece has to do is motivate your viewer to take action. You need to make them want to call for more information, visit your website, or just come into your store. Invite them to take action on every page.
To motivate customers to act, you can:

- ➤ Offer special "bonus" offers to quick responders
- ➤ Make a time-sensitive offer
- ➤ Tell them how rare your product is, or what limited quantity you have

> ➢ Offer limited-time added value

Are you telling them what your product or service will give them?

Your customer doesn't care about the features of your product or service, they only care about the benefit that feature will provide them. Customers buy benefits, not products or services. A client is looking to buy some more confidence from a new hairstyle, not a haircut.

Are you telling viewers the story of your product or service?

Remember that you are painting a story to tap into the emotions of your viewers. Detailed technical descriptions should be replaced with descriptions of how the customer may enjoy the benefit, and how they might feel.

The story will help the reader picture:

> ➢ How they'll feel after using your product or service
> ➢ What they'll look like using your product or service
> ➢ What they'll have time to do once they buy your product or service
> ➢ The relief they'll experience after purchasing your product or service

Are you giving them a reason to keep your marketing piece?

Give your customers a reason to keep your business card, brochure, newsletter or direct mail piece, refer to it, and pass it on to others to see. For example, Colm Rogers of One Stop Printing (www.OneStopPrinting.ie) is someone who I work closely with on a number of projects and Colm has one marketing piece that is a premium spot UV varnish 300gsm brochure that you wouldn't dare throw out.

The Truth!

If you are selling hair care products, you can give your readers tips on how to combat split ends, frizz, unruly curls and heat damage. If you sell kitchen products, you can provide recipes that use your cookware or tools.

Some ideas for keep-able marketing pieces are:

- Top 10 lists
- Tips for product caretaking and longevity
- Recipes
- How-to's

Flashy design is not important to your marketing campaign - but clear and professional looking materials are absolutely essential.

When it comes to the visual presentation of your marketing materials, you need to strike a balance. On one hand, you don't want to spend your entire budget on design and production. On the other hand, the cost of sending out materials that don't look and feel professional is usually much higher.

If you're going to try something new - test, measure and make mistakes in small batches, or online.

You will need to constantly be monitoring the success of each piece of marketing material and looking for opportunities to strengthen and improve it. Since you already have your lead tracking and management system in place, this is a matter of sitting down on a regular basis and reviewing the leads each piece generated, and how many turned into sales (we'll review this when we get to conversion rates.

Remember, always test, measure and then make choices.
If you're not sure about a new strategy, do a test run to a limited distribution area, or test the message out online. Do small production runs of brochures or flyers you're not sure

about, so you don't end up with heaps of flyers that didn't work.

In the end, the strength of your marketing piece is in what you say and how you say it.

Read that again

Too often, flashy design gets in the way of the message and you miss an opportunity to attract a customer. Simple, clear marketing materials deliver an easy-to-understand message to your target audience, and result

The next chapter will look at the role of your offer in motivating your audience to take action. A powerful - even irresistible - offer can act as an ace in the hole for your lead generation efforts. I'll show you how to put one together.

The Truth!

Crafting Powerful Offers That Compel Action

"Anything that is measured and watched, improves."

- Bob Parsons

Focus on using powerful offers to generate leads, not to close sales.

Powerful offers that drive your audience to take action can be used in your business to do a myriad of things. They're great for moving old or overstocked product, overcoming buyer objections, eliminating purchase risk, or even just building your customer database.

Well-crafted offers are also fantastic lead generators - which is what we're going to focus on in this chapter. In this case, the offer is designed to get potential customers to identify themselves, not to close sales. Once those potential customers have identified themselves - they've taken action to redeem the offer - they enter the formal sales process and you can convert them into a loyal customer.

Offers designed to be lead generators drive more qualified prospects to your business. They weed out the buyers who would take advantage of your offer, but who are not otherwise a part of your target market.

I'm going to show you how to speak to your target market's "hot buttons" and emotional motivators, instead of simply crafting an offer based on financial savings or bonuses. Let's get started!

In this chapter we will cover:

> ➤ The elements that make an offer 'powerful'
> ➤ A step-by-step process for creating a powerful offer
> ➤ Types of powerful offers
> ➤ Examples of powerful offers
> ➤ Testing and measuring your powerful offers
> ➤ A powerful offer is irresistible to your potential customers' emotional motivators.

In simple terms, a powerful offer gets people to respond, or take action. It will provide enough motivation for the reader to pick up the phone, visit your website, or walk into your store.

Often, powerful offers are called irresistible offers because they seem too good to pass up. They make your target audience think, "Wow! This is the chance I've been waiting for!" or, "I'd be nuts not to take advantage of this opportunity!"

Using emotional motivators in your offer (and in your headlines and copywriting) will drive qualified prospects to your business, and will make the job of converting customers into repeat business easier and more cost effective.

A powerful offer will feature an element of urgency or scarcity as a key motivator for action.

If I was a hair and beauty salon owner and offered "2 for 1 Mother Daughter haircuts" every day of the year, chances are I wouldn't have a stampede of prospects at my door. I would likely draw a few new clients a week, but the majority of those who saw the offer - even if they were interested - would probably put it off for later.

When you create an offer for lead generation, you want your prospect to take action as soon as possible. Now, let's face it, we're all procrastinators at heart, so you have to give your audience a reason to take action without delay.

So, instead of just "2 *for 1 Mother Daughter haircuts*" I could offer, "2 *for 1 Mother Daughter haircuts, Mother's Day weekend - 20 spots available, book your appointment today!*" This offer has an element of urgency - the offer is only valid for a two-day period - and scarcity - there are a limited number of appointments during those two days.

Here are some other ways I could use scarcity or urgency to 'sweeten' the offer:

Strategy	Scarcity / Urgency	Example
Limited time offer	Urgency	2 for 1 Mother Daughter haircuts - Mondays from 1pm to 4pm.
Limited supplies available	Scarcity	Free! Mother's Day gift (€50 value) with purchase for the first 20 customers on Mother's Day.
Seasonal specials	Urgency	Mother's Day Special: buy one; get one free on any service in our spa, Mother's Day weekend only.
Free gift with action	Scarcity	Bring your mom in for a free haircut on Mother's Day, and receive a salon bonus pack, worth €45, absolutely free!
Daily deal	Urgency	Book an appointment with us by the end of the day, and we'll add on a free haircut for your daughter.

Let's walk through an easy step-by-step process for creating powerful offers that will generate qualified leads for your business.

1. Establish who you are trying to target and what you want them to do.

Like all of your lead generation efforts, you need to establish who your target market or audience is before you can attempt to reach them. In most cases, this will be the target market you originally identified. In my salon example, the target market is middle-class women aged 18 to 65 with an interest in the latest trends in fashion and beauty.

You may also wish to segment that group of people into a more specific category. I could limit my target audience to those women in my target market with daughters.

Secondly, you must be clear about what you want your readers to do, and ask them to do it in your offer. Since you're creating an offer to generate leads, in this case you want readers to identify themselves in some way, and make contact with you. In my example above, I asked customers to call and reserve their appointment today. You may ask your readers to come to the store for a free trial, or place an online order.

2. Identify the emotional motivators or "hot buttons" that will get your target to take action.

Using the categories below, decide why your target market needs or wants what you have to offer. How do they feel in general about your product or service? What problem does your offer provide the solution to?

- ➢ Safety and financial security for self and family
- ➢ Convenience and time management
- ➢ Freedom from worry
- ➢ Self-improvement

- ➢ Acceptance and recognition from others
- ➢ Basic needs, including food, shelter, love, personal maintenance, etc.

In the example above, I'm targeting the emotions associated with the bond between mothers and daughters, especially on Mother's Day, and their common interest in beauty services.

The offer alludes to an opportunity to spend time with each other, an activity for Mother's Day, and a way to save money while doing so.

3. Once you have identified the emotions you will try to target, determine which type of offer will work best.

Free Offer:
Ask your potential customer to act immediately for a free reward. This is a great lead generator if you can offer a solution to a common problem for free. Examples would be "Contact me now to receive your free 10-page guide to financial freedom," or "Act now and get your first month of home security for free - a €99 value!" Try to include the monetary value of what you are providing for free to increase the perceived value.

Guarantee Offer:
Guarantee the performance of your product or results of your service and you'll take away the fear many customers feel when making a purchase. This is a great way to overcome barriers when a customer is making a large or important purchase, or when safety and security are involved.

- ➢ Money-back guarantee: full refund for unsatisfied customers.
- ➢ Double-your-money-back guarantee: double refund for unsatisfied customers.
- ➢ Long-term guarantee: one year, multi-year or lifetime guarantee.

Free Trial or Demonstration Offer:

Another great way to reverse purchase risk is to offer a free trial or €1 trial (7, 14, or 30 days) or to provide a free demonstration. This works with all kinds of products or services, and allows the customer to convince himself that he needs what you have to offer. Those customers who are concerned about making the right purchase decision will be put at ease by this offer.

Package or Value-Added Offer:

This offer appeals to customers looking for convenience because their needs are met in one place or one purchase, like start-up kits and special packages. Packaging products also increases the perception of value, often without adding costs. For example, offering a free printer with computer purchase.

Premium Offer:

Always offer premiums over discounts, as they will better serve your bottom line. Reward purchases with bonus products or services, and you'll give new customers an incentive for choosing your business over the competition.

4. Draft several hard-to-refuse offers based on these motivators.

Brainstorm as many different types of offers as you can, using emotional keywords or hot buttons. Depending on the type of business you have, and the products or services you offer, you may wish to focus on a single product or service, or open up the offer to all the items you have in store.

Are there any freebies you can throw in? Any overstock that can be handed out as a free gift, packaged with a complementary product? What about bonus services that you can add on to products for a limited time (with limited costs)? Will a simple guarantee make a big difference?

The Truth!

Remember that when you are describing your offer, be as specific as possible and avoid lengthy description of product details and benefits. Your goal is to sell the offer and motivate readers to take the next step, not to sell your product.

5. Evaluate the financial viability of each of your brainstormed offers.

Even though you're using these offers as lead generation tools, you need to make sure that each transaction will turn an acceptable profit - or at least allow you to break even. The last thing you want to have happen is a store full of leads redeeming an outrageous offer that will leave you broke.

So, for each of your brainstormed offers, calculate your break-even point. If I were offering 2 for 1 Mother Daughter haircuts, my calculation would look something like this:

A. Costs: Determine the costs involved in your offer (hard costs - product or service, and soft costs - advertising or marketing).

Service costs:
Adult Haircut: €20
Junior Haircut: €10

Marketing costs:
Advertising: €200
Flyer Drop: €100

B. Profit: Assess how much profit you'll generate per sale (price minus hard costs).

Adult Haircut: €40 (price) - €20 (cost) = €20 profit
Junior Haircut: €0 (offered free) - €10 (cost) = €10 expense

Profit: €20 - €10 = €10 profit per transaction

C. Break Even Point: Calculate how many transactions you'll need to break even (how much profit will you need to make to cover soft costs).

Advertising (total): €300
Profit: €10
Transactions: €300 / €10 = 30 transactions required to break even.

From here you can assess whether or not you can realistically break even, and if your offer is financially viable. In this example, 30 transactions is a reachable target for the salon over the course of a weekend. They may also consider extending the offer over the course of a week, maintaining an element of urgency, but allowing more time to recover my costs.

Keep in mind that their initial purchase in response to your offer may only allow you to break even, but if you are able to convert them into repeat customers, the profit of their subsequent purchases may make up the difference.

6. Select two of your financially viable offers, then test them to measure which works best.

I like to test two offers at a time when I first start to use this lead generation strategy. This will tell me what emotional motivators really work with my target audience, and then I can continue to build on that knowledge.

Use your lead tracking system to measure which offers generate the highest number of leads. If coupons are a part of your offer, put a tracking code on each of them, or make sure that your staff are asking every inquiry which offer they are responding to.

Remember, testing and measuring is a vital component of your lead generation efforts, and it elicits some really valuable information. Once you know what works with your audience, you can use that information on emotional motivators to influence decisions you make when writing headlines and other copy.

Get creative and put together new and exciting offers for your potential clients on a regular basis.

Remember - you'll need to keep improving and revising your offers to ensure you continue to draw leads from them. Otherwise, your audience will get used to seeing the same offer, assume it is always available, and it may become stale.

Use opportunities like seasons, events, anniversaries and other celebrations to change and renew offers. When you bring in a new product line, feature a new service, or try to go after a new segment of your target market, check-in to see if you can create an offer around the news and bring in some new leads.

In the next chapter, we're going to spend some time cultivating your headline writing skills. You'll see that we use headlines in all types of marketing and sales materials, and they're a powerful - or even essential - component of your lead generation tools.

John Mulry, MSc

Writing Headlines That Demand Attention

"As long as you're going to be thinking anyway, think big."

- Donald Trump

All your headline needs to do is convince your reader to keep reading.

Just like your lead generating offer, your headline has one job. It doesn't need to close sales, or win copywriting awards, it just needs to grab and hold your reader's attention long enough to keep them reading.

Studies have shown that around 80% of people read headlines when they're looking through the newspaper, but only about 20% actually read the ad or article.

Your headline is the only tool you have to get the rest of your copy read, so you'll need to focus the majority of your copywriting efforts on catching and holding your readers' attention. The rest of your copy only matters if you can get them to read it!

In this chapter we will cover:

> The role of strong headlines in all of your marketing materials
> Headlines as emotional motivators
> How to create strong headlines for your audience
> Examples of strong headlines
> Headline templates
> Testing and measuring headlines

Headlines shouldn't be limited to advertising alone - they're essential elements of sales letters, direct mail cards, websites, newsletters and brochures. Headlines are used to grab and

134

hold reader's attention in ALL marketing materials - not just advertisements in newspapers.

Most readers take only a few seconds to decide if they want to spend any time reading what you have to say, in an email, website, sales letter or direct mail postcard. Just like you, your audience is bombarded by information every minute of the day, so if you haven't convinced them to care in a few seconds or less, they've already moved on.

As we discussed, your sub-headline is almost as important, because it's your second chance to tell the reader why they should care and keep their attention. It also creates a transition between your headline and the body of your letter or advertisement, and acts as a teaser.

Every headline should:

> ➤ Grab the reader's attention
> ➤ Be something the reader cares about
> ➤ Offer your reader something
> ➤ Trigger emotional reactions
> ➤ Incite curiosity

Headlines need to trigger an emotional response and motivate your reader to keep reading.

When you're writing, you have to put yourself in the mindset of your audience. People are pressed for time, so your headline has to offer something to them that is going to solve their problem, make their life easier, or give them information that they know they need. Otherwise, they've already turned the page.

For example, if I were to write a headline like this – *"Give me three hours of your time and I'll show you how to double your annual income by creating a passive income stream"* - I'm probably targeting overworked, overwhelmed, underpaid professionals who are struggling to provide for their families. I've tapped into their emotional motivators and caught their attention.

There are a few categories of basic human needs that most purchase motivations come from. When you are aware of these, you will be able to incorporate them into your writing and appeal to your target market's emotions.

By identifying your target market's needs, wants, and desires, you'll be able to identify the words and phrases that will effectively trigger emotional reactions, which will motivate them to take action.

Using the list of basic human needs below, identify which apply to your target market and create a list of words that will trigger the emotions related to these needs, wants and desires.

- ➢ Personal, financial and emotional security for self and family
- ➢ Convenience and time management
- ➢ Freedom from worry, including peace of mind, comfort
- ➢ Self-improvement, including spiritual, intellectual, physical
- ➢ Acceptance and recognition from others, including self esteem, achievement, attention, respect, companionship
- ➢ Basic needs, including food, shelter, clothing, love, personal maintenance

When you begin writing your headlines, you will discover that certain word combinations are also very powerful. You can combine your list of emotional trigger words with these power words in all of your copywriting.

According to a Yale University study, the top two rows of words are the most powerful words in the English language.

The Truth!

Love	Money	Health	Discovery	Proven	Save
Safety	You	Easy	Results	New	Guaranteed
Breakthrough	Profits	Discover	Incredible	Shocking	Shocked
Ultimate	Free	Master	Uncovered	Hidden	Secret
Revealed	Scientific	Your	Powerful	Suddenly	Miracle
Now	Magic	Announcing	Offer	Introducing	Quick
Improvement	Amazing	Wanted	Sensational	Challenge	Remarkable
Compare	Startling	Bargain	Hurry		

Here's how you can write effective headlines for your business in a few easy steps.

1. Identify who you are trying to target.

You need a clear understanding of who you're writing for and what their motivators are before you can attempt to reach them. This is the target market you identified for yourself in the target market chapter.

If you are trying to target a more specific group within your target market, you can chose to segment your market into sub-markets by demographic or behavioristic characteristics. For example, you might choose to focus on only men or only women with children under five years of age.

The more specific you can be with your market, the easier time you will have identifying and reaching their emotional 'hot buttons.'

2. Identify what you are trying to communicate.

Once you know who you're speaking to, clearly define what message you need to communicate to them. Be specific, and even write it down in plain language before you start drafting your headlines.

To clearly articulate your message, ask yourself questions like:

- ➢ Do you have a solution to their problem?
- ➢ Do you offer a new product or service that they need?
- ➢ Can you provide the information they're looking for?
- ➢ Do you have a better option for them?

3. Identify the motivators or "hot buttons" that will elicit an emotional response from your audience.
Take the list you drafted above, and highlight or write down the words that will pique your target market's interest, or trigger their 'hot buttons'.

If you're selling vacuum cleaners to young mothers, you're going to want to identify words that would appeal to her desire to keep her home germ free for toddlers, and make her cleaning efforts easier and less time consuming.

When you're writing for sales and marketing, always try to paint a picture for your audience. Carefully select descriptive words they will relate to and resonate with, and strong power words like the ones listed above. For example, phrases like "challenging outdoor experiences" would appeal to physically fit readers, but not those who don't like to exercise.

4. Choose a type of headline that will work best based on the emotional motivators you have identified.

Direct Headlines clearly and simply state the offer or message, without any attempt at humor or cleverness.

Pure Silk Scarves - 40% This Weekend Only | Brand New Security System Just €99 Per Month

Indirect Headlines are subtle, and often use curiosity to pique a reader's interest before providing an explanation in the body copy. Clever puns, figures of speech and double meanings are often used. The key to weight loss success lies in your backyard.

News Headlines mimic a headline you would read in the newspaper and are a great option for a new product announcement or industry scoop. These work best when you actually have news, and can stay focused on benefits, not features. Mummy Madness launches the ultimate timesaver for new moms

Question Headlines ask the reader something they can closely relate to or would need to continue reading to discover the answer. Questions are easy to read, and can immediately tap into your reader's emotions.

Are you tired of worrying about your children's education fund? | Do you know what's in your fruits and vegetables?

'How to' Headlines indicate that the rest of the copy or the offer itself will describe a step-by-step process of interest or use to the reader. These two words create headlines that work wonders.

How to find a job in a recession | How to start a profitable internet business from scratch.

Command Headlines are similar to direct headlines, but always start with a strong verb or command for action. It usually focuses on the most important benefit you offer your reader.

Triple your energy in just three days | Stop wasting money when you travel.

'Reasons Why' or 'Ways to' Headlines precede lists of tips, suggestions, product benefits or even mistakes of interest to your target audience. Keep the list to a reasonable length or you'll run the risk of losing your reader.

Eight ways to save money around the house | 25 mistakes you could be making at the grocery store.

Testimonial Headlines use other people's opinions and expertise to persuade a reader to keep reading and begin to build trust. Quotation marks are used to indicate that the words are a testimonial, not the words of your business, and they can increase readership by almost 30%.

"XYZ Bootcamp completely changed the way I look at my body" - Miley Cirrus | "I never thought I'd get out of debt before I discovered Money Saver XYZ!" - Grace LePage

5. Draft at least ten different headlines using the templates below, and pick your best three to test and measure.

I often get asked how long a headline should be. This is something that is debated in the marketing community quite a bit, but I always tell my clients not to stress about it. Use the number of words you need to get your point across, without writing a paragraph. Remember that your headline needs to do one thing: get the reader to keep reading.

Don't be afraid to draft pages of headlines or sift through the pages of a thesaurus before you get yours just right. Sometimes you're only a word or two away from transforming a boring headline into a really effective one. If you're having trouble, you can rely on the headline templates I've included below

Headline Templates:

How to become the smartest _____ in _____
How to end _____
How I improved my _____
How to develop _____
Seven ways to add to your _____ without cleaning out your bank account
How to begin _____
12 innovations in _____ design
How to enjoy _____
Introducing the four key rules for _____
How I _____
Six things to check when buying a new _____
How to conquer _____

Complete these three simple steps for a _____
How to start_____
Five hints to make your _____ rise above the rest
How to have_____
How to become _____
Announcing eight powerful answers to your "what _____ to buy" dilemma
Which _____ do the experts use?
Powerful ways to update your _____ for free
How to keep _____
The four components that make up a successful _____
How to improve your _____
Six essential questions to ask before you buy a _____
How to get _____
Three clever ways to impress _____ without breaking the bank
The six warning signs you don't want to miss in _____
How to get the most out of _____
Nine tips from the _____ experts
How to avoid _____
How to stay ahead of business _____ trends in _____
How to get rid of _____
Five proven advantages that _____ enjoys over the competition
How you can _____
Finally! The latest _____ secrets revealed!
Learn how xxx has improved since you bought your last _____

6. Always test and measure the effectiveness of your headlines.

Try two at a time and compare which generates the best results. As always, you will need to test and measure the strength of your headlines. Try to test at least two "hot buttons" in different media to determine where your target audience's reaction is the strongest.

You can leverage off of the information gathered from testing and measuring your powerful offer as well. For example, if the offer geared to safety and security concerns was a roaring success, headlines that tap into those motivators will also be successful.

You can apply these headline writing techniques to all your marketing materials, as well as your copywriting.

In our fast-paced society, nearly everyone has become a skimmer instead of a reader. Strong, well-written headlines are the only way you can lure a browser into reading your message - so use them on every piece of marketing material you have.

Final Thoughts...

"If you're not a risk taker, you should get the hell out of business."

- Ray Kroc

Interrupt, engage, educate, and offer make up the marketing equation, and that equation should be the backbone of all the incredibly successful marketing campaigns you'll put together. You can probably tell from the depth of information in this book that I have a bona fide step by step system that helps business owners just like you use superior marketing that makes your phone ring. Remember earlier I said that this system works for big, Fortune 500 kinds of companies. Well, my passion doesn't lie with helping huge, soulless corporations.

My passion is for you, the business owners who are, in my opinion, the real people running this country and every country for that matter. You're the guy or gal who is up every morning, risking it all, putting up with the crap day in day out.

I offered my system to you in this book as a way to reach the ultimate pinnacle of life: freedom for you and your family... along with the ability to do whatever you want with your time and money. After all, you more than likely started your business because you have a true passion yourself for what you do. But when your marketing is ineffective, owning your own business can become no more than working a poorly paying job.

Compelling and successful marketing can provide you with the financial freedom to pursue your real, true ambitions in life.

I believe that everybody has a cause, a cause that can be more fully pursued and supported when you're financially independent. Let me help you reach that goal. I have the tools, resources and support to help you accomplish this in record time. All I ask if that you give me a chance to show you how effective our marketing can be for your company.

Bonus: Why Do Top Performers Use Coaches?
By Dan S. Kennedy

When Arnold Palmer needed to "tune-up" his game, to compensate for his age, he sought out a 26 year old 'swing coach'. Everybody who follows golf knows about the troubles Tiger had with his game after parting with his coach, Butch Harmon. We know most athletes in every sport use coaches, personal trainers and sports psychologists. But do sales professionals and entrepreneurs need coaches too?

Having personally had over 200 high-flying entrepreneurs, small business owners, salespeople and self-employed professional participate in my coaching groups and tele-coaching programs over the past 8 years — some for all 8 years, and been the coach and advisor to nearly 100 business coaches in different fields, I think I have a pretty good understanding of why coaching seems to work so well for entrepreneurs, and why you might want a coach of your own. There are six reasons:

- Being Held Accountable
- Being Questioned And Challenged
- Being Listened To
- Being Recognized For Your Achievements
- Being Accepted
- Being Motivated

Different people have different needs at different times in their lives, but I find most entrepreneurs share all six of these to varying degrees.

The Truth!

Accountability

On many occasions, as a speaker, I was on programs with, and had private "green room" time with legendary athletes like Joe Montana, Troy Aikman, Olympian Mary Lou Retton, George Foreman, and coaches like Tom Landry, Lou Holtz, and Jimmy Johnson. The athletes all agreed that high performers personally hold themselves to gruelingly high standards, but even so, were it not for feeling accountable to teammates, fans and coaches, and being held accountable by their coach or coaches, who monitored their statistics, replayed film of misjudgments and mistakes, analyzed and assessed their performance, they would never have reached the levels of success they did.

The joke of entrepreneurship is: good news and bad news. You're your own boss! Having a coach guide you in committing to doing, changing, testing certain things between now and the next call or meeting, then having you report on those things is guaranteed to improve your follow-through on your own best ideas! In short, accountability automatically improves performance and results.

Questioned and Challenged

The more successful you are the less likely the people who work for you or are around all the time are to challenge your ideas. It's easy to wind up surrounded by "yes men." The outside coach with no axe to grind can be both objective and force you to defend your ideas. If you can, that's valuable. If you can't, that's valuable too.

Listened To

A Newsweek magazine article about professional business/life coaches described us as "part therapist, part consultant." A lot of entrepreneurs have no one to talk to about business OR personal matters who dare "let their hair down with"… who will listen without any agenda. I often find that a client will talk his way to his own terrific answer, solution, or plan of action if I'll just listen. Having a coach with life and business experience relevant to your own, who is personally successful, who can relate to is extremely beneficial.

Being Recognized For Your Achievements

Everybody needs recognition and celebration — but to whom can the entrepreneur brag? Certainly not to his employees, his competitors, his vendors. Since most of the people the coaches and I advise worth with are "Renegades," using unorthodox marketing strategies, most the people around them actually disapprove of a lot what's working, even if they grudgingly acknowledge the results.

And often, if the owner of the business takes the garish black on neon green oversize postcard he spent days slaving over that just pulled a 14 to 1 ROI home to show his wife and kids, he gets a very disinterested response. A "That's nice, dear" — not a "Holy crap! 14-1! You're a genius! Can I get a copy of that?"

Having a knowledgeable coach, or better yet, being a part of a coaching/mastermind group gives everyone of us an appreciative audience who "gets it", who understands our accomplishments, and is able and willing to celebrate our achievements because they are secure in their own success.

Being Accepted

I call most my successful clients (and myself) "Renegade Millionaires" because we violate just about every norm of our industries and professions... we are actually quite dysfunctional in one way or another... we think and talk differently than almost everyone around us in our day to day lives. Because of this, a lot of success entrepreneurs actually suffer silent frustration and loneliness. In many instances, we can't even explain what we do to 'civilians'! Feeling like "the fish out of water" most of one's waking hours is not all that pleasant. That's why being a part of a coaching/mastermind group with like-minded 'Renegades' is so invigorating. One of the core human needs is to be accepted for who you are, without need of mask or cautious editing of expressed thought.

Being Motivated

Surely a top pro athlete being paid millions of dollars to play a game doesn't need "motivated—" but, actually the fact that they are paid millions, win-lose- or -draw, means they do need a great deal of other motivation to do all the behind-the-scenes hard work required for peak performances on the field.

In almost every locker room, after every game, grown men who are paid millions to play their games are awarded game balls. Coached cry, hug, 'atta boy!', nudge.

Ultimately, all motivation is self-motivation, but there's definitely contributions made by the people and ideas you associate with, the involvements you're in, the successes of others you're exposed to.

What Exactly is Business Coaching?

Most of the industry-specific advisors I work with deliver coaching much the same as I do; with different 'levels' appropriate for different people.

The most common options begin with simple group teleseminars or classes often with open question/answer for the participants, sometimes support with website resources or communities.

Next, all that plus periodic mastermind group meetings. At the highest levels, people travel from all over the country to attend the meetings. I created local Dan Kennedy "Study Groups" combining education, Mastermind meetings, and Coaching facilitated by a 'Certified No BS Business Advisor' in each city. Information about YOUR Local Glazer-Kennedy Chapter Mastermind programs can be obtained by sending an email to John Mulry at John@JohnMulry.com

………………..

Why Should You Plug-In' to John's Glazer-Kennedy Insider's Circle Chapter Mastermind & Coaching Programs?

If any or all of the six needs I described apply to you, then the best investment you'll ever make is finding and joining one or several appropriate coaching programs!

To find out more about joining John's coaching, monthly group and *'the place for prosperity'* visit www.GKIC.ie

A Special Invitation From John

Dear friend and reader,

Thank you for reading this short book. I hope you found it beneficial and that it sheds new light on how you will market your business in this new economy.

Would you like me to work with you personally to turn your 'successful-but-stuck' business into a MORE systematic, scalable, profitable machine that has you attracting more clients, have them coming back more often and referring more business your way than ever before?

Have you heard the phrase: *"action breeds success"*? Well it's very true. You've taken the first step, are you willing to take a couple more? If you are, I'm willing to set aside some time for you personally.

During that time, I'll evaluate where you are in your business now, and where you want to get to. I'll show how to increase your sales and profits and using my '5 Profit Pillar' formula for success. Chances are there is a pocket of under-served customers, clients or untapped potential in your business. I'll work together with you to map out an immediate action plan you can take to profit from them.

There is no charge and no catch.

Why am I doing this? Great question, my reason is twofold:

1. I genuinely enjoy working with forward thinking, successful business owners that are always looking to improve themselves and their business.

2. Some people who have this marketing strategy 'kick start' session with me become clients. If you feel you get value, we

can discuss working together long term.

Oh by the way, our strategy session will in no way be a sales pitch in disguise. I will not pressure you, bother you or force you to become a client in any way.

To apply for your kick-start session visit:

www.JohnMulry.com/wrong

P.s. I must mention, I'll be asking you some 'thought provoking questions' when you visit that link above. These alone will definitely get you thinking differently about your business. And sometimes, a different perspective is all you need.

Also From the Author

Your Elephant's Under Threat:

John's highly acclaimed first book details his journey from lost, alone, with no direction and living someone else's life to drawing upon the transformative power of positive change within him and the others he surrounded himself with. He changed his life, found happiness, has a business that serves him and now with the information, systems and strategies he shares in this self improvement book, you can too....

Praise for Your Elephant's Under Threat:

"If you're an entrepreneur who's struggling to adapt to the changing world of business or you need a system for defining and getting exactly what you want in life, then you need this book."

- **Brian Tracy International, Legendary Speaker, Trainer and Author of over 60 Best Selling Books**

"The thing about John that most people aren't willing to do, is to actually APPLY the best practices that they learn to their own business and life in order to achieve maximum effectiveness in minimum time. I love the fact that John lives and breathes what he teaches in this book. One of the most important concepts that surfaces in his book is summarized in his three words: INVEST, CONSUME and ACT. If ever there was a simple definition of how to succeed, John has 'nailed it' with these words. Moreover, he's living proof that the invest/consume/act model works."

- **Nick Nanton, CEO of the Dicks + Nanton Celebrity Branding® Agency, Emmy Award Winning Director,**

Producer & Best-Selling Author

"In order to achieve success in life, you must first expect it, define it, and apply knowledge gained through education and experience. John Mulry's book, Your Elephant's Under Threat, is an excellent tool to use on your journey."
- **Tom Hopkins International, Speaker and Author of How to Master the Art of Selling**

"What a fantastic, straightforward, and honest book backed by a WONDERFUL story of positive change. If you are an ambitious entrepreneur and want to have your own story of personal triumph and business success, read this book!"

- **Clate Mask, CEO and Co-Founder of InfusionSoft**

"John Mulry's personal story and journey is provocative and profound…He has revealed a lot about personal and business transformation, making it an organised process rather than an accidental evolution."

- **Dan Kennedy, Author & Marketing/Business Strategist**

For more testimonials and to get your copy visit:
www.JohnMulry.com/elephant

Prologue to Your Elephant's Under Threat

"CHOOSE not to accept the false boundaries and limitations created by the past."

– Unknown

One Bite at a Time

One bite at a time. That's what they tell us. That's how we're supposed to do it. Tackle our problems, I mean. Achieve our goals. We need to break the big, massive problem into small, manageable, bite-size chunks.

You know the saying, "How do you eat an elephant? One bite at a time." And it works. Most of the time.

I'm a problem solver at heart – I guess that's why I am in the business of helping people. It's my calling. I guess it's why I love the world of personal development so much. The notion of breaking down a problem – be it an abstract equation or a problem in life or business – into manageable chunks seems doable. Most of the time.

There's that phrase again, *most of the time*. There are two problems with our elephants and two problems with the bite-size problem-solving formula.

First problem: Elephants never forget. Have you ever had a goal that, no matter what you tried, you just couldn't achieve it? Even if you tried to break it down to the smallest chunks possible? Me, too. It's really frustrating. You start to feel like a failure, like you're not moving forward, like you're regressing instead of progressing.

It's not because you're stupid, it's not because you don't have the time, energy, or resources; it's because your goal or elephant, if you may, is under threat. A threat that won't be forgotten and one that must be addressed.

That elephant you want to break into manageable chunks won't be broken down until you identify the threat behind it that's stopping you from achieving. From there, it's all about Defining, Refining, and Aligning, as Dax Moy calls it.

The second problem with elephants is they're easily conditioned. Let me illustrate with a story. You may have heard of this one. It's not new. It's the story about the elephant and the tether. I first came across this story while devouring every book and seminar by the charismatic and wonderfully talented Tom Hopkins.

A family is out on a day trip to the zoo. It's a glorious summer day and the clear, blue sky is cloudless. The family – a mother, a father, and two young kids – are going from enclosure to enclosure, soaking up the spectacular views of the animals and their antics.

They come upon the elephant enclosure and the father is suddenly on edge. The enclosure is only secured by a measly wire fence and the giant elephant inside is kept there by a small rope held in place by an even smaller wooden stake.

Fearful for his children's safety, he calls over the zookeeper and exclaims, "How on earth can you keep that elephant from going on a rampage and harming little kids?"

The zookeeper laughs and says, "The elephant isn't going anywhere. It's tied down."

"But it's only a thin piece of rope; even I could break free from that," the father says.

"Sure you could, but the elephant can't," the zookeeper replies in a smug voice.

"How can that be?" the father asks.

The Truth!

The zookeeper proceeds to tell the family that when the baby elephants are first put into the enclosure, they are kept there by a big, massive chain that's connected to an even bigger rock.

The baby elephant tugs and tugs at the rope all day, every day but never breaks free. After about six months, it gives up. Completely. At this stage, the zookeepers remove the big chain and rock and replace it with the thin piece of rope and small wooden stake.

To the elephant, it's the same thing. It doesn't matter what's keeping him tied down because he's never going to break free. Why? Because he doesn't believe he can. He's been conditioned to believe he'll never be able to do so.

The same goes for all of us. We all have similar tethers or threats in our own lives that prevent us from moving forward, from living the life we deserve, having a body we can be proud of, and running a business that serves us.

The tethers and threats in our lives aren't just belief-related, either. Other threats can be fear-based, including fear of failure, fear of judgement, fear of commitment, and even fear of success. Anything that holds us back is exactly like the stake keeping the elephant tied down. No matter what size it may be in reality, it's the affect it has on our ability to act that matters most.

Until we address the tethers or threats in our lives, we will never break free and will always be like the elephant that's tied down.

This book aims to help you realise that the threat holding you back in your life and in your business is merely a small piece of rope. I aim to show you that it is one which *you* have the power and answers inside to break free from permanently.

To get your copy of Your Elephant's Under Threat visit: www.expectsuccess.ie